I0477011

SWEAR WORD
COLORING BOOK

AN ADULT COLORING BOOK OF 40 HILARIOUS, RUDE AND FUNNY SWEARING AND CURSING DESIGNS

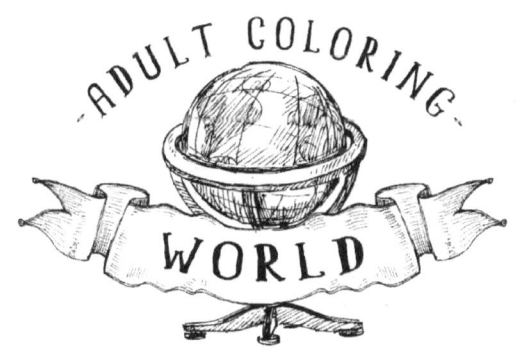

Copyright © 2016 Adult Coloring World
All rights reserved.

ISBN-13: 978-1523312696
ISBN-10: 1523312696

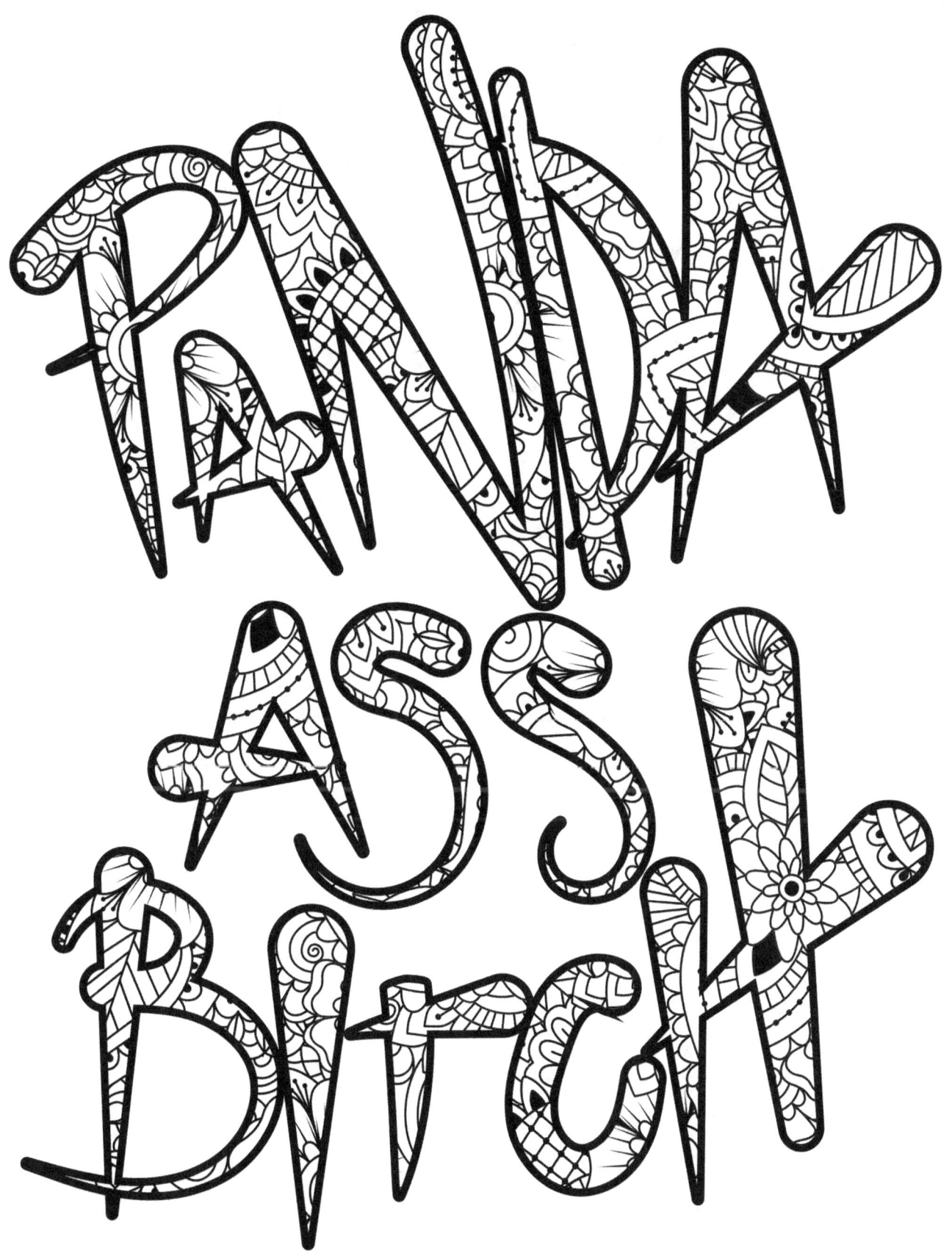

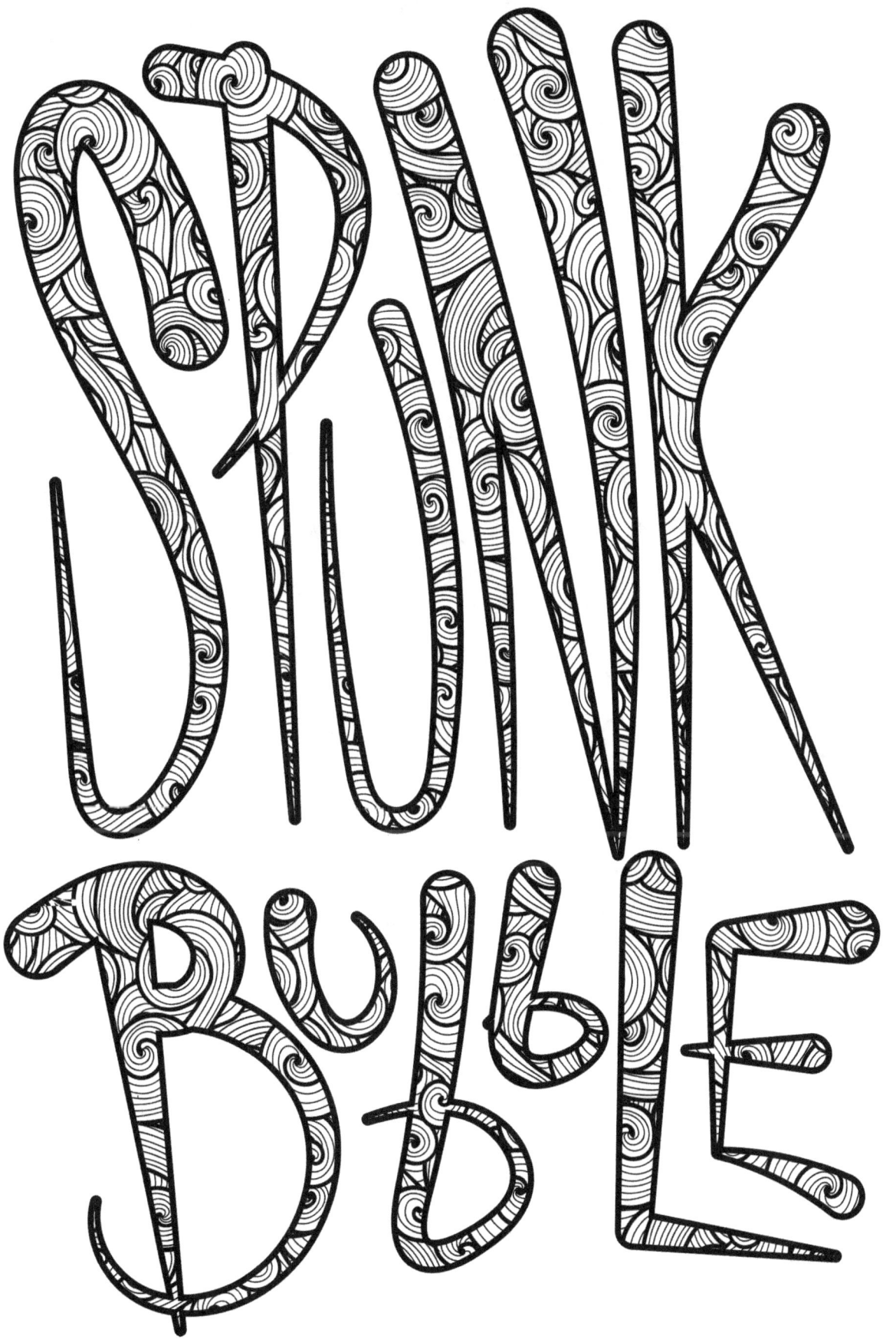

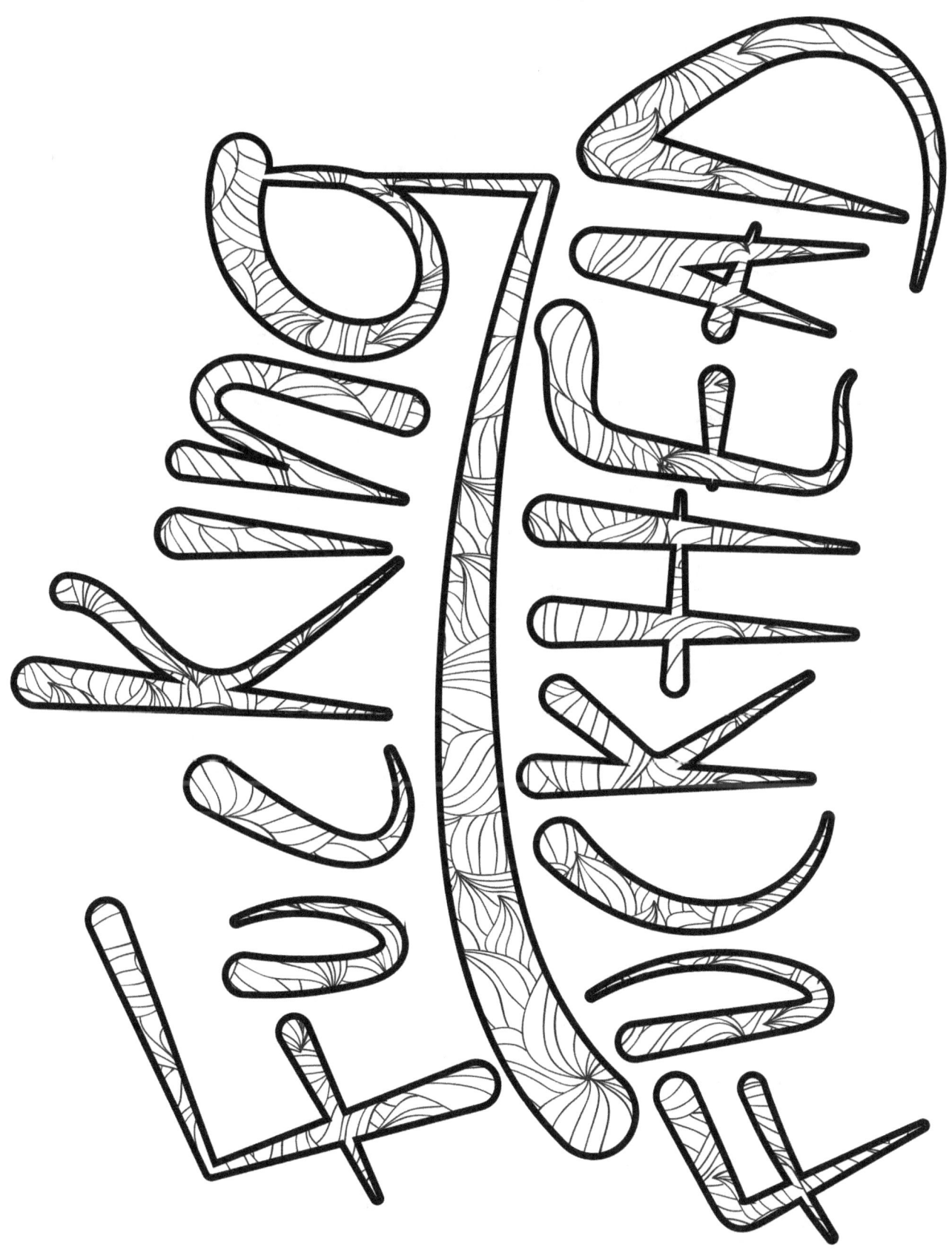

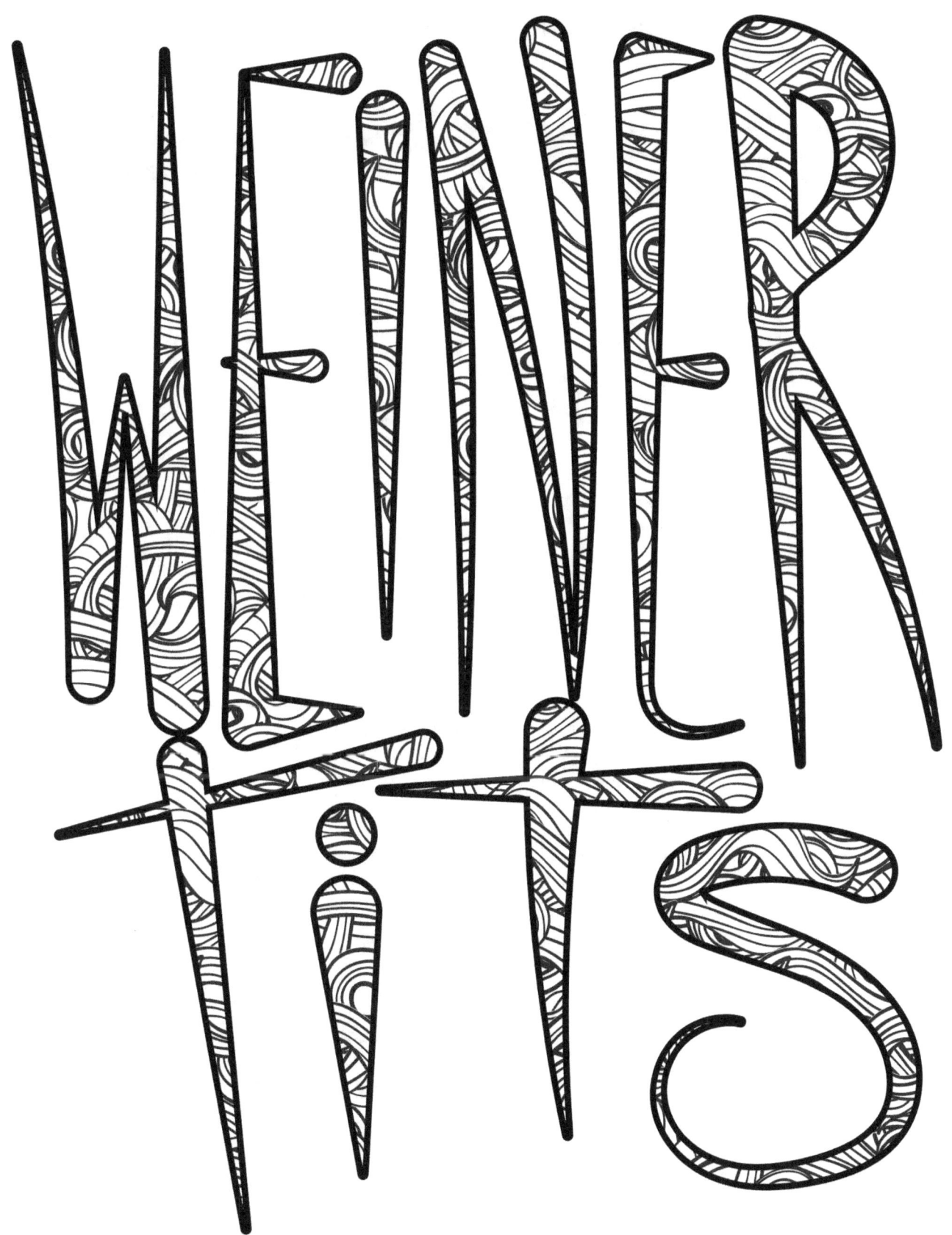

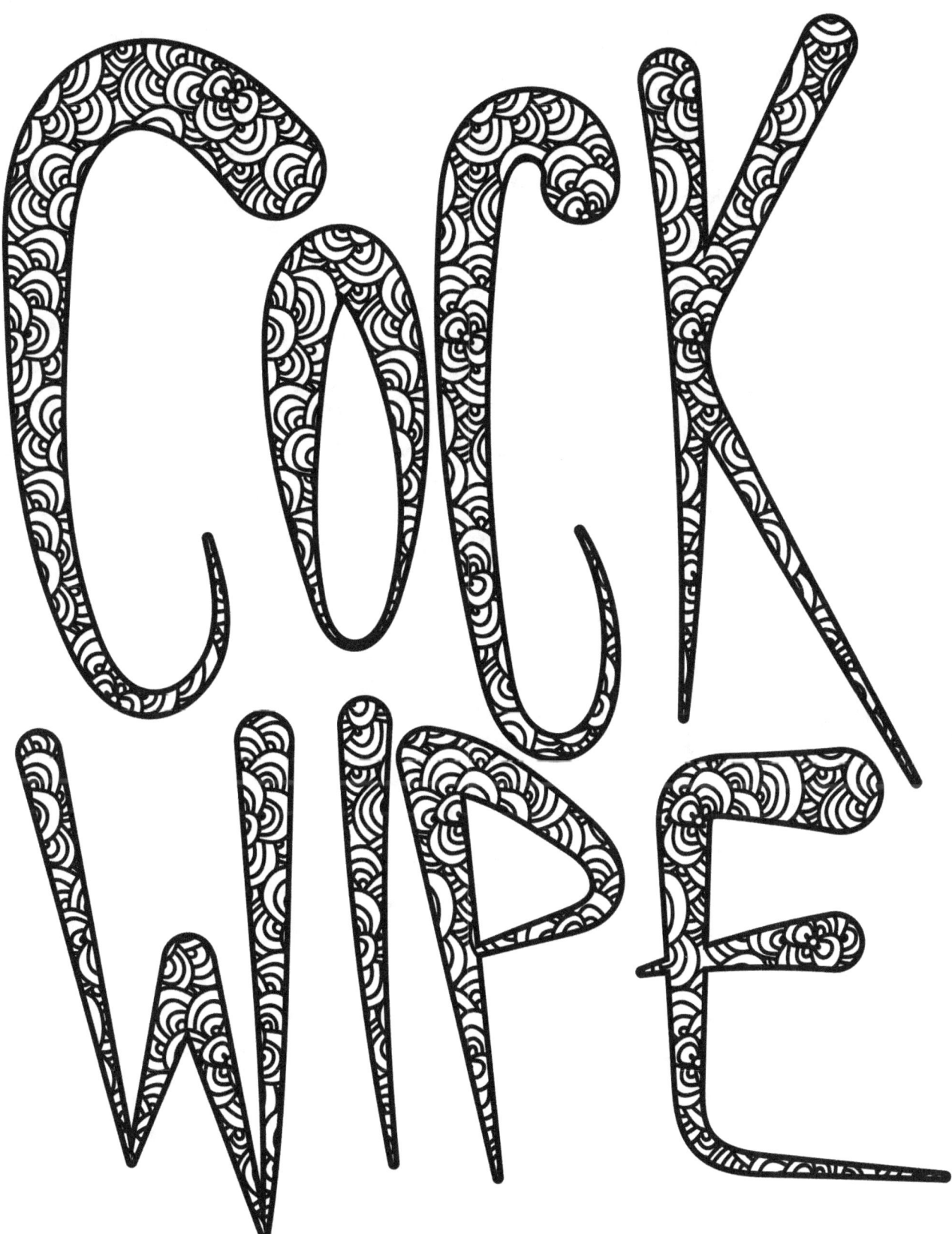

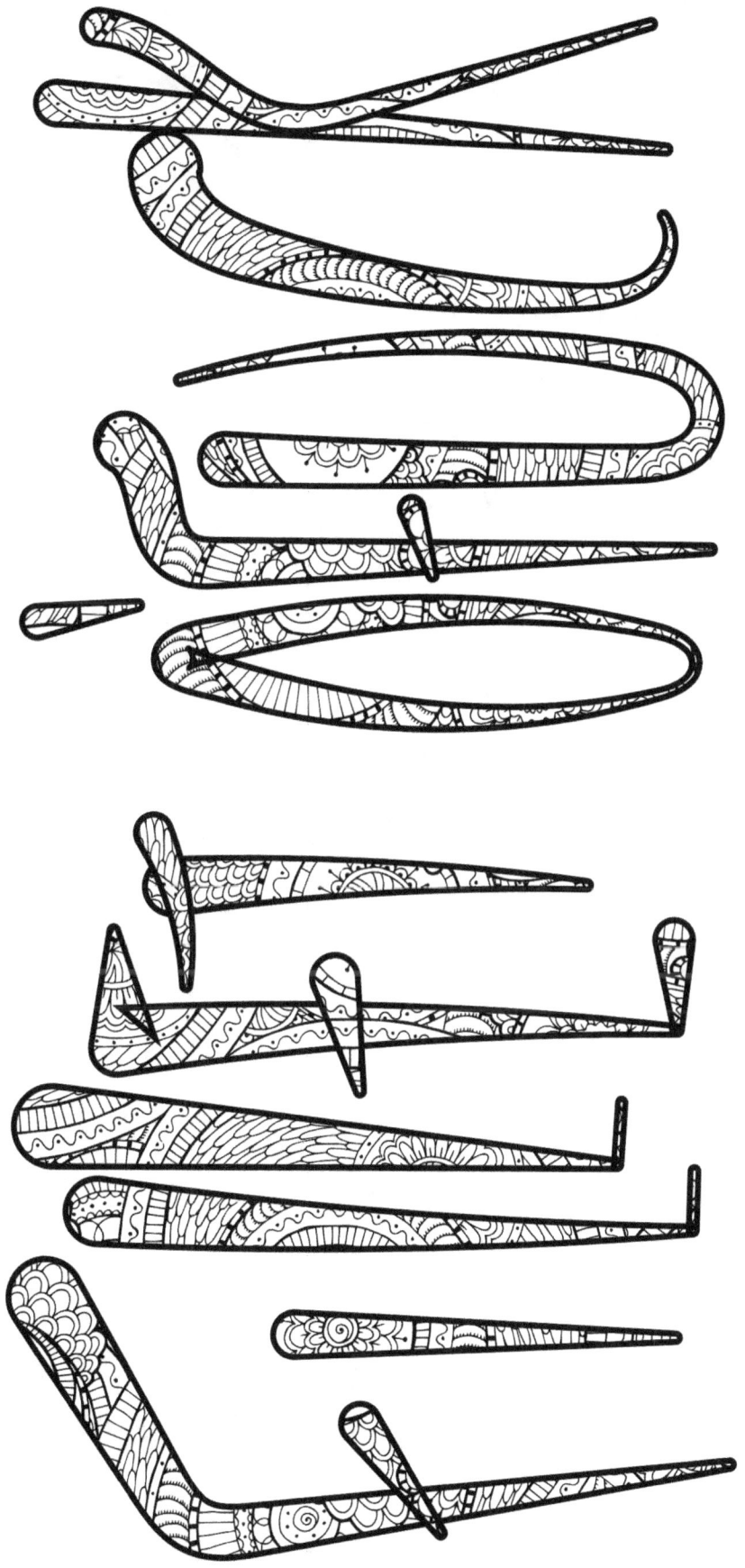

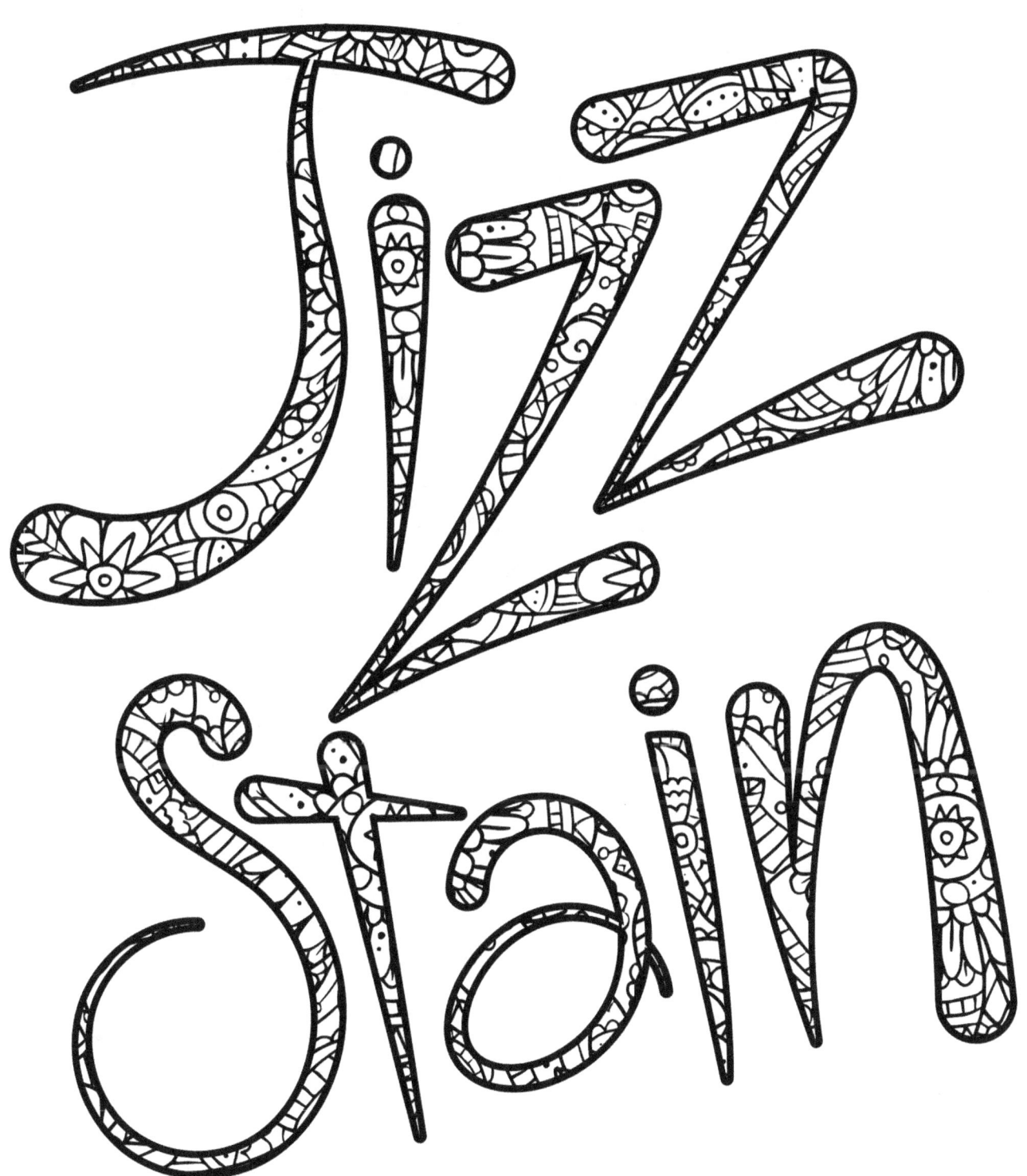

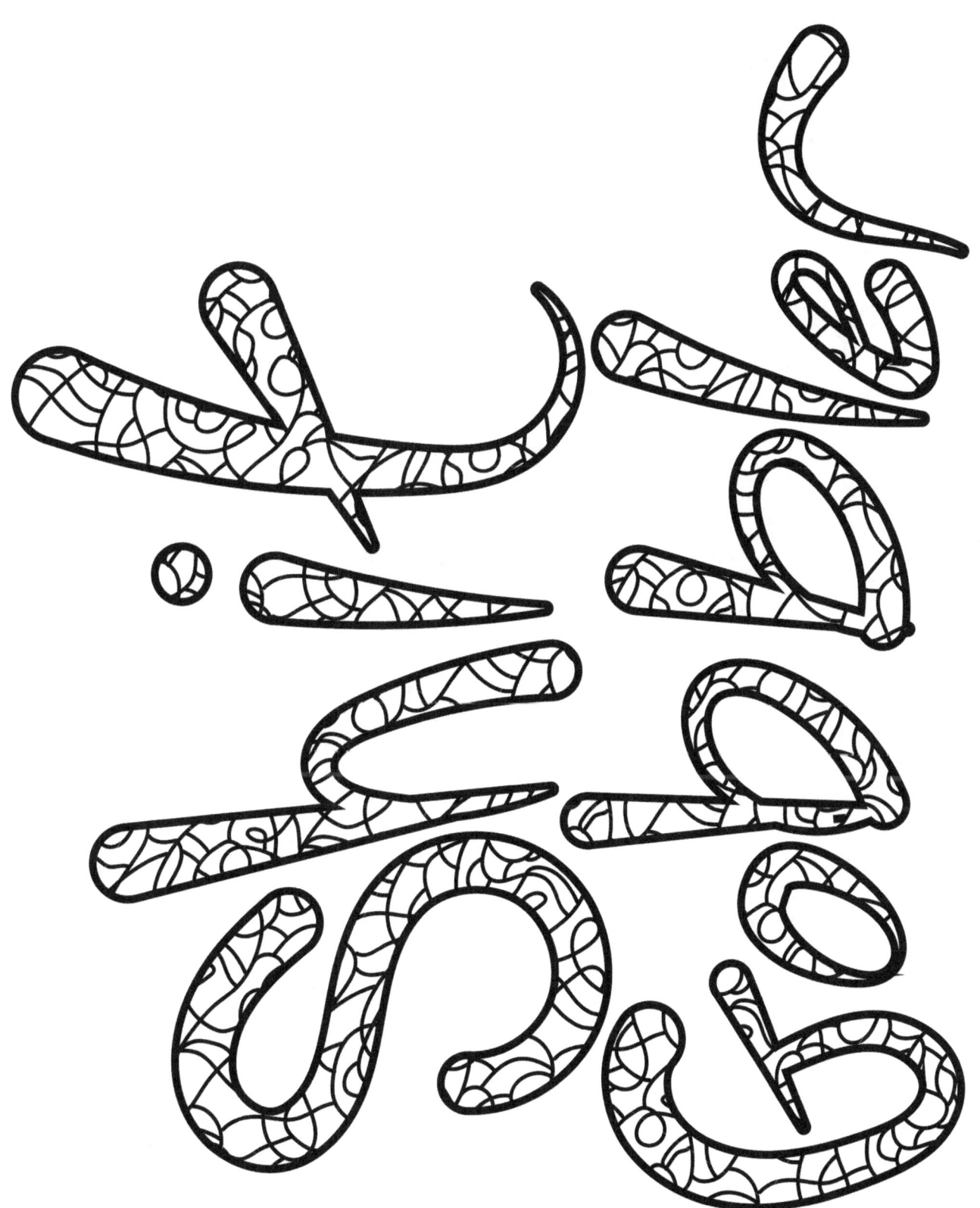

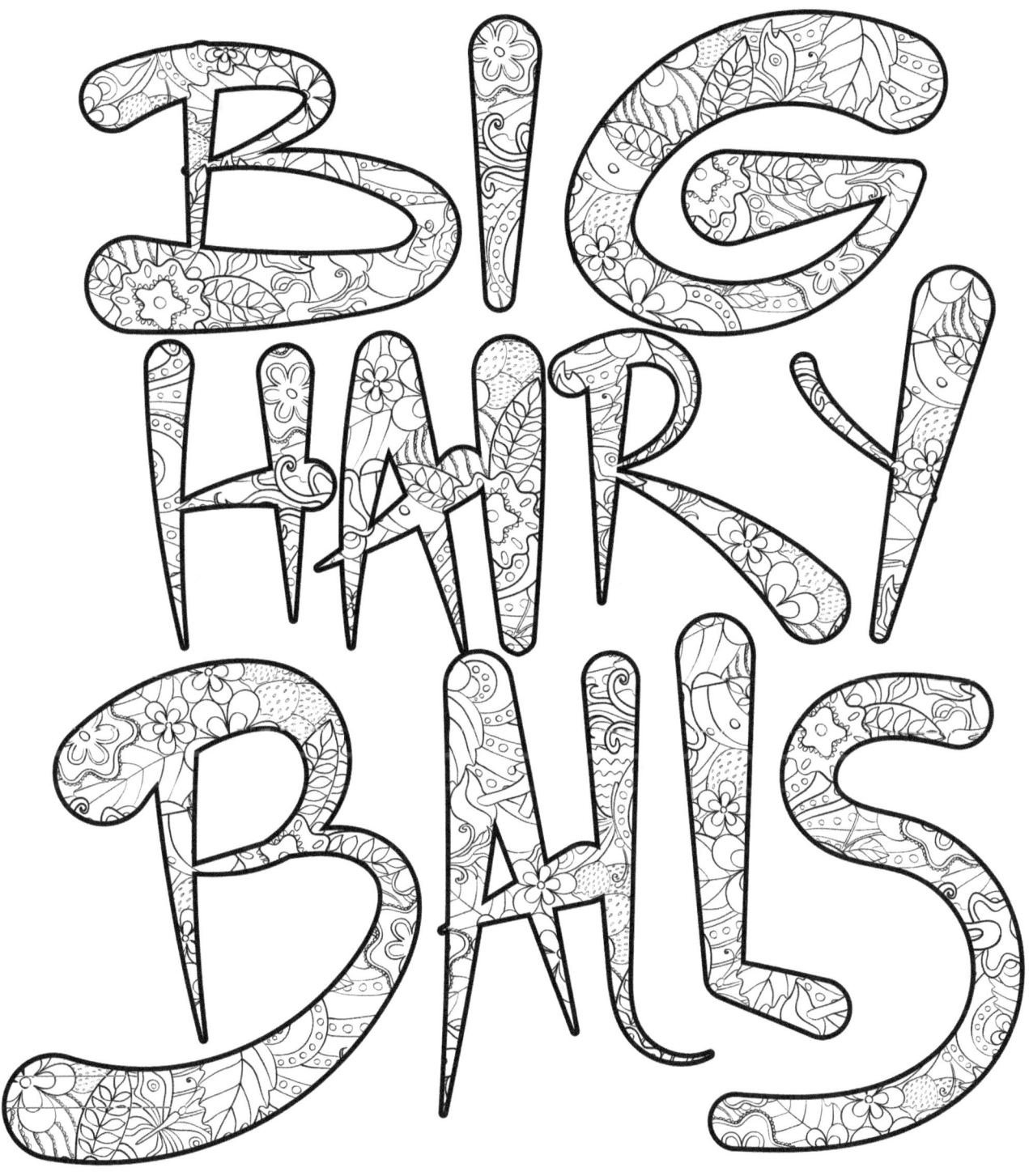

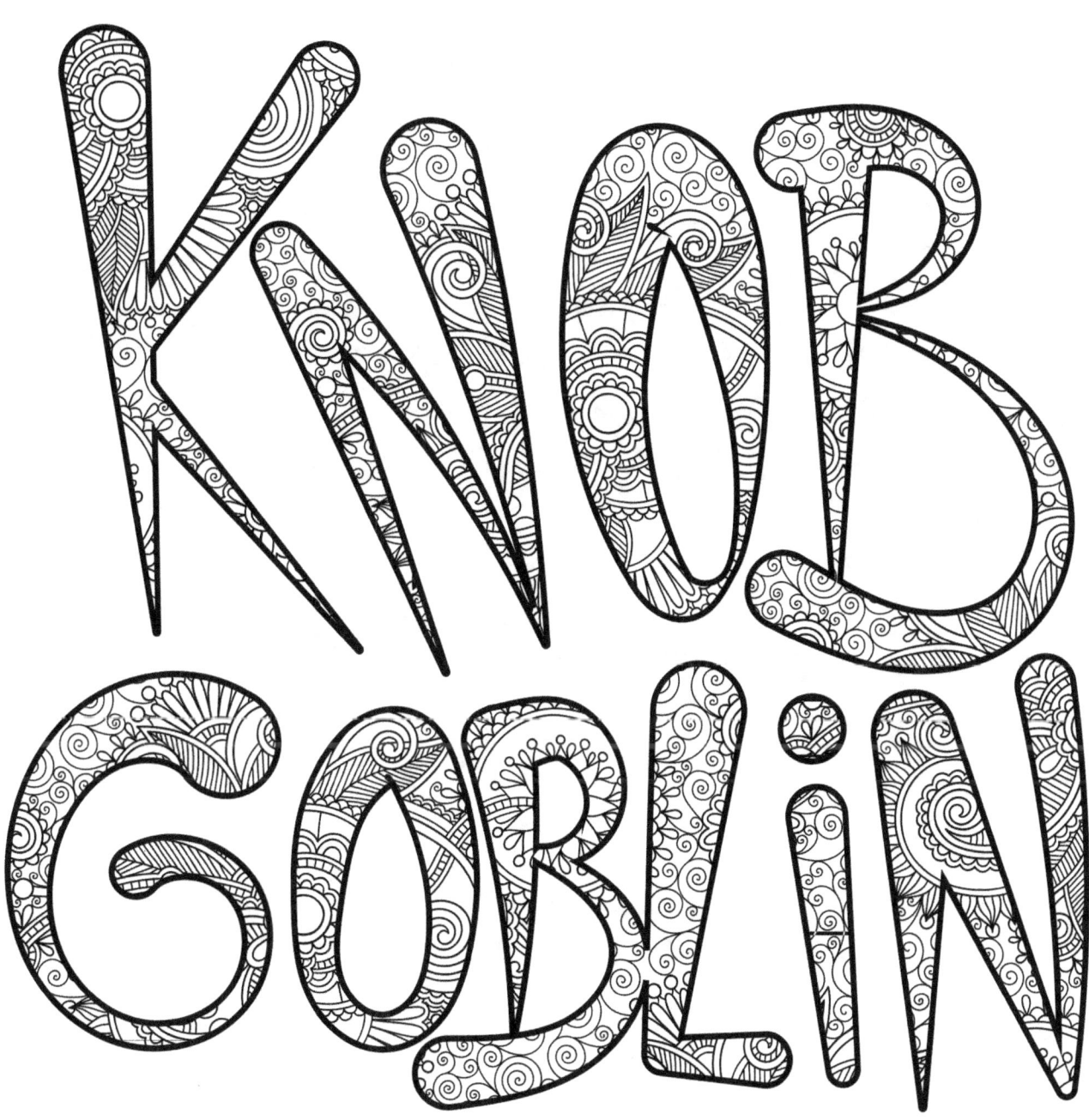

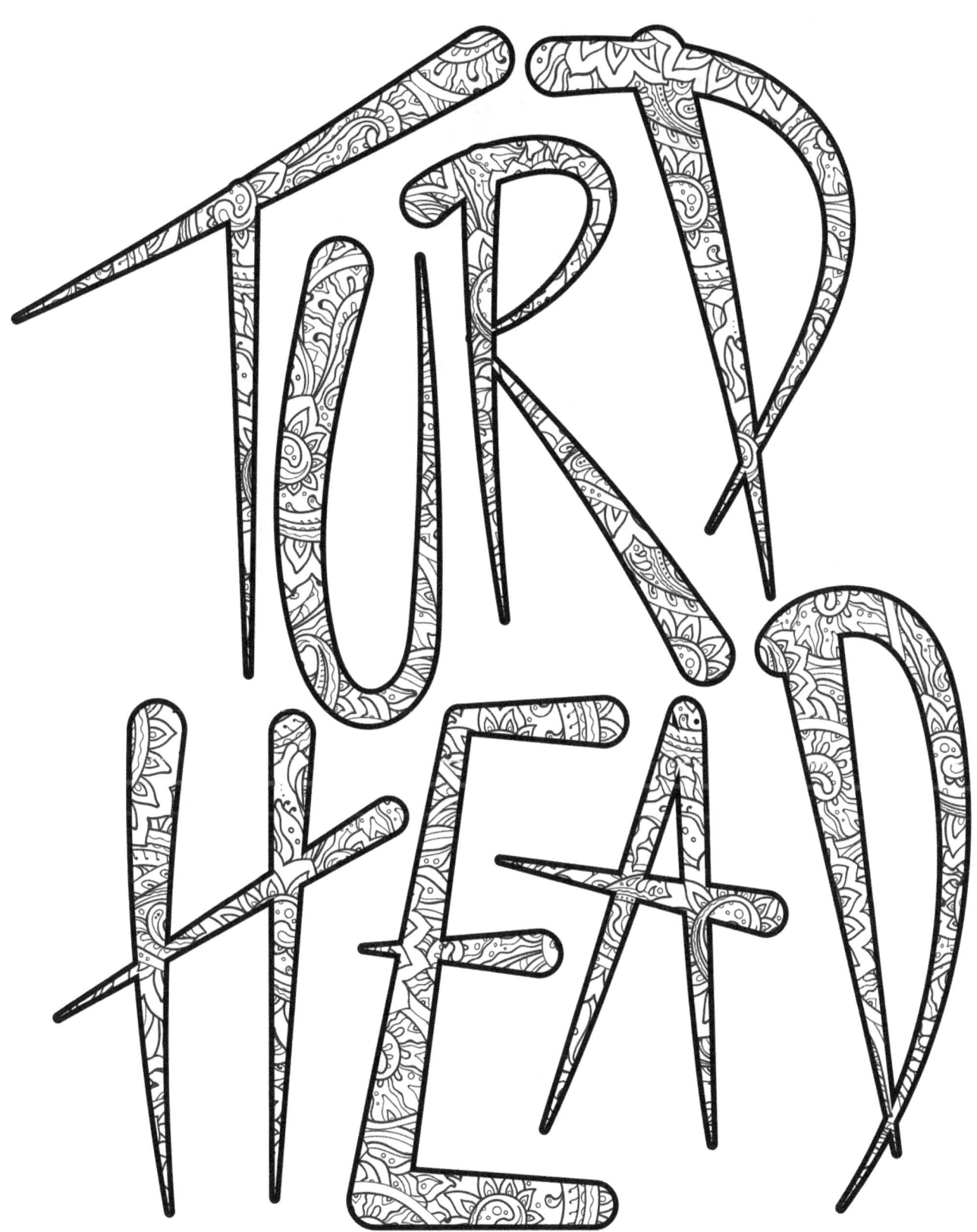

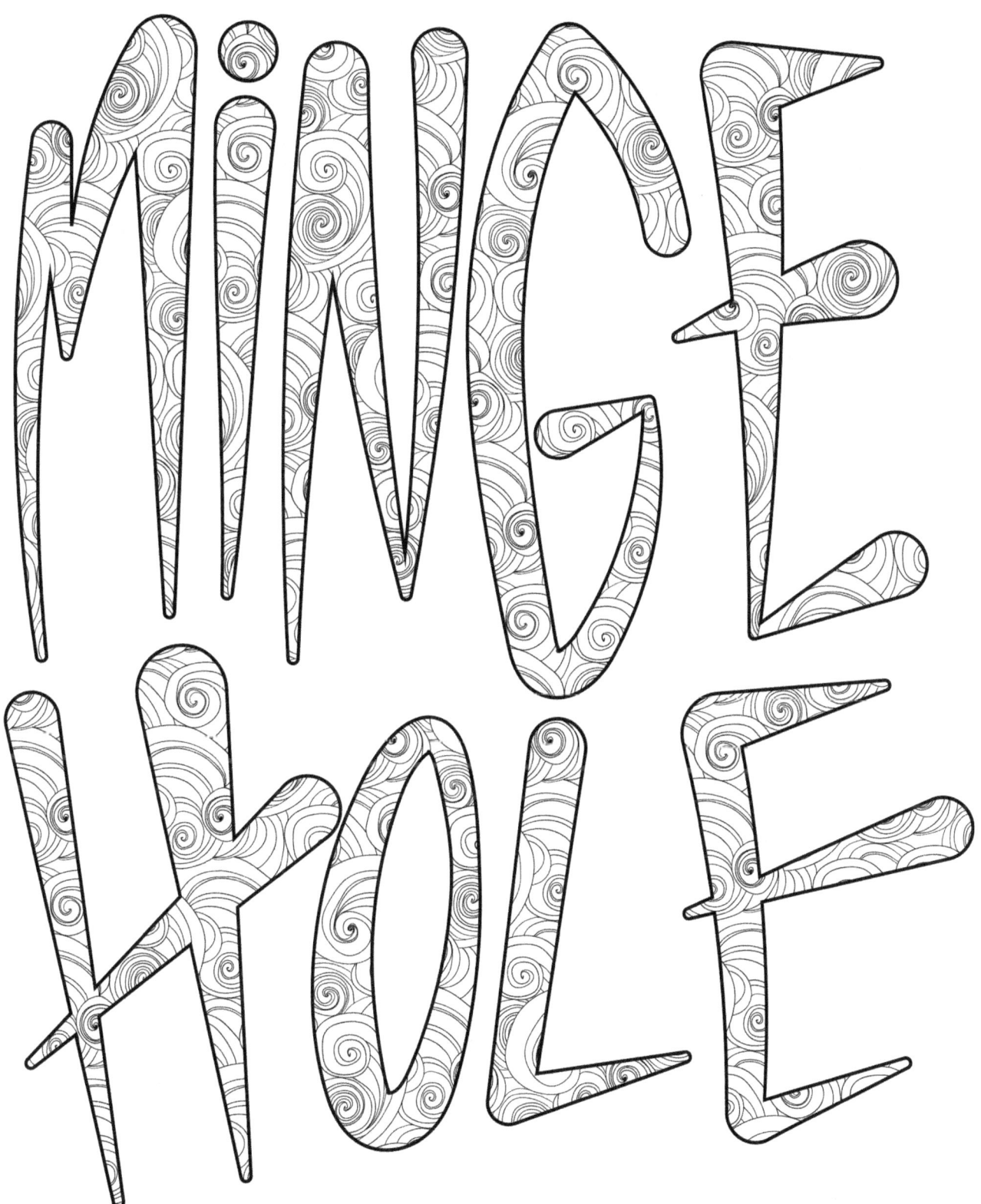

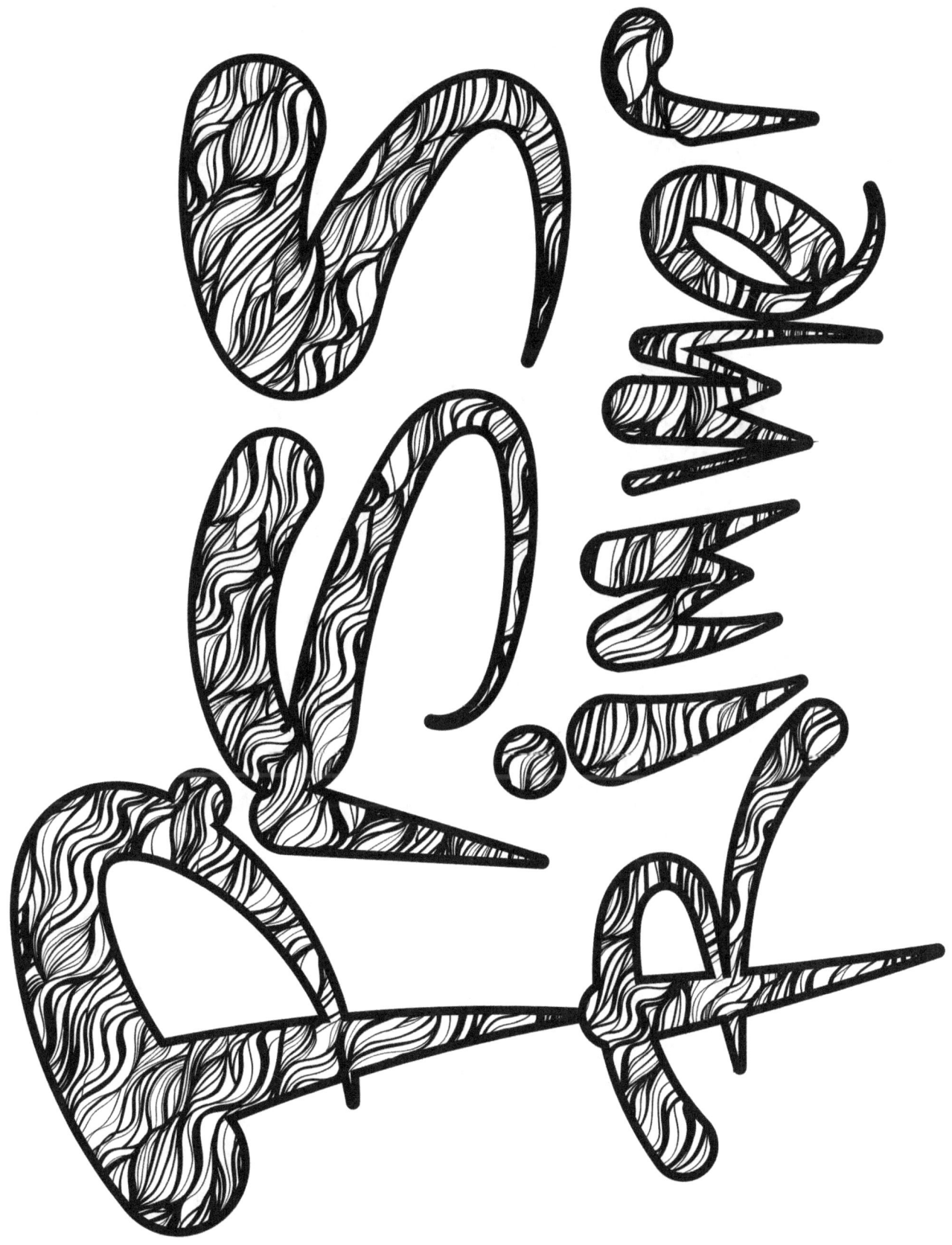

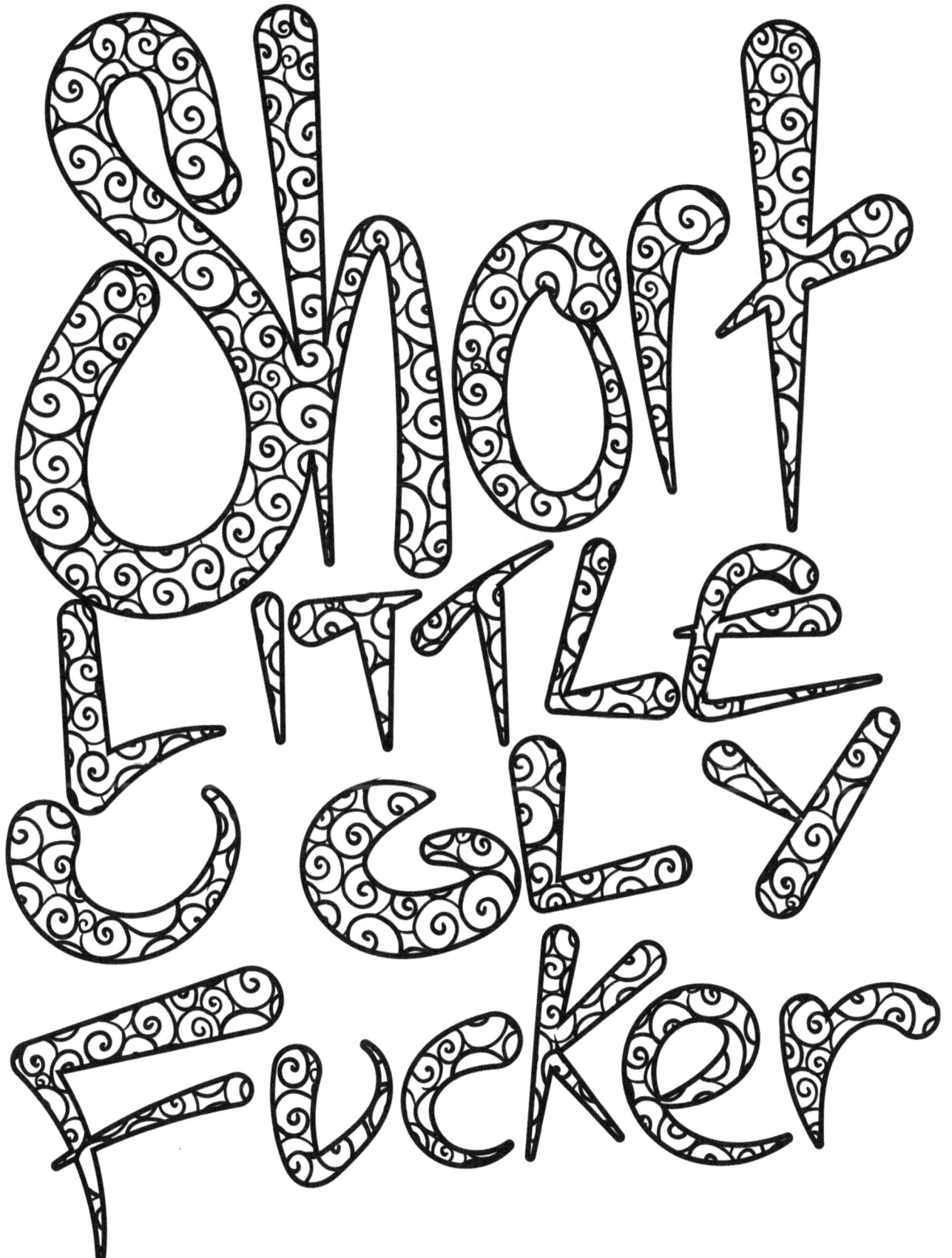

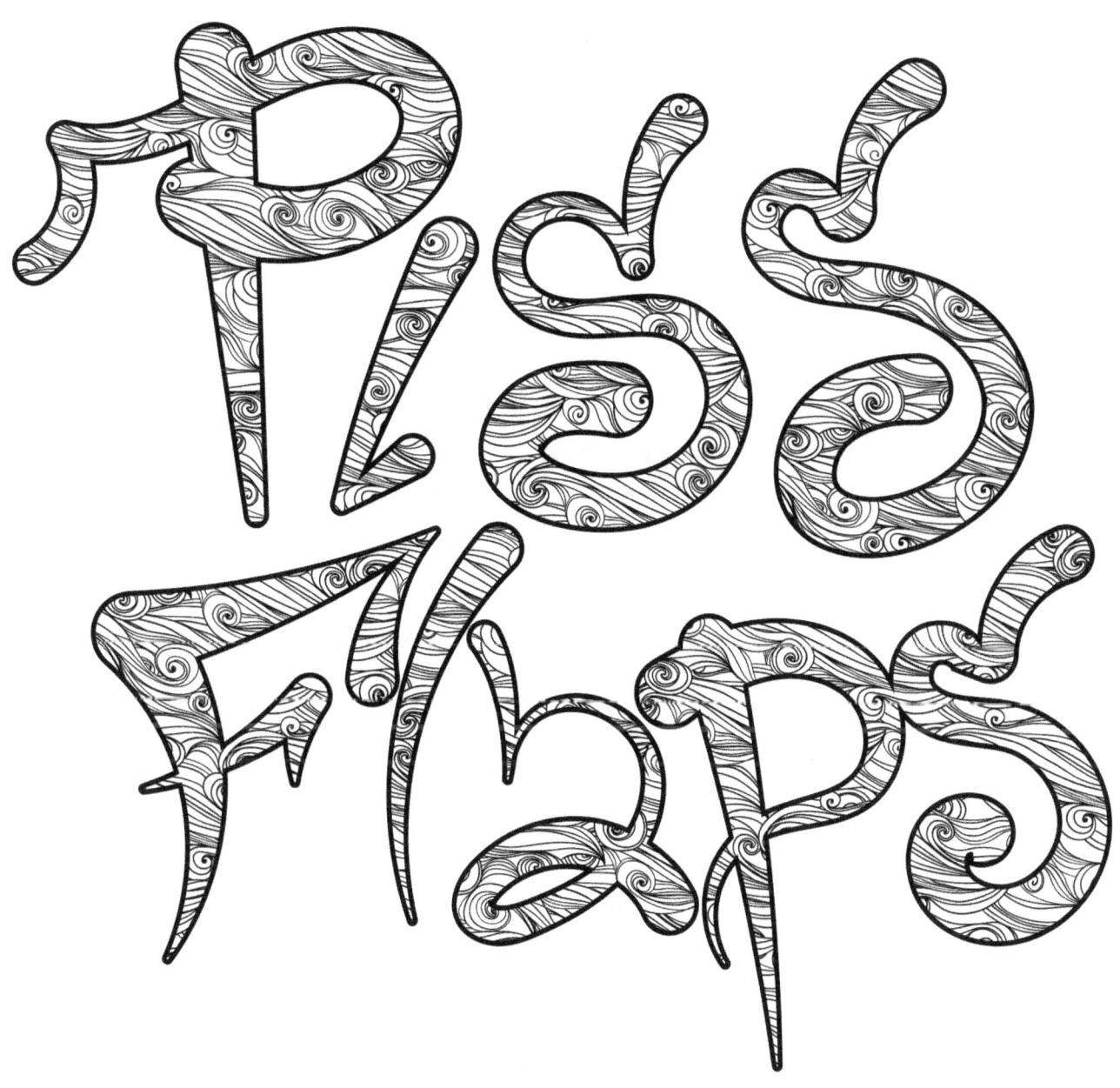

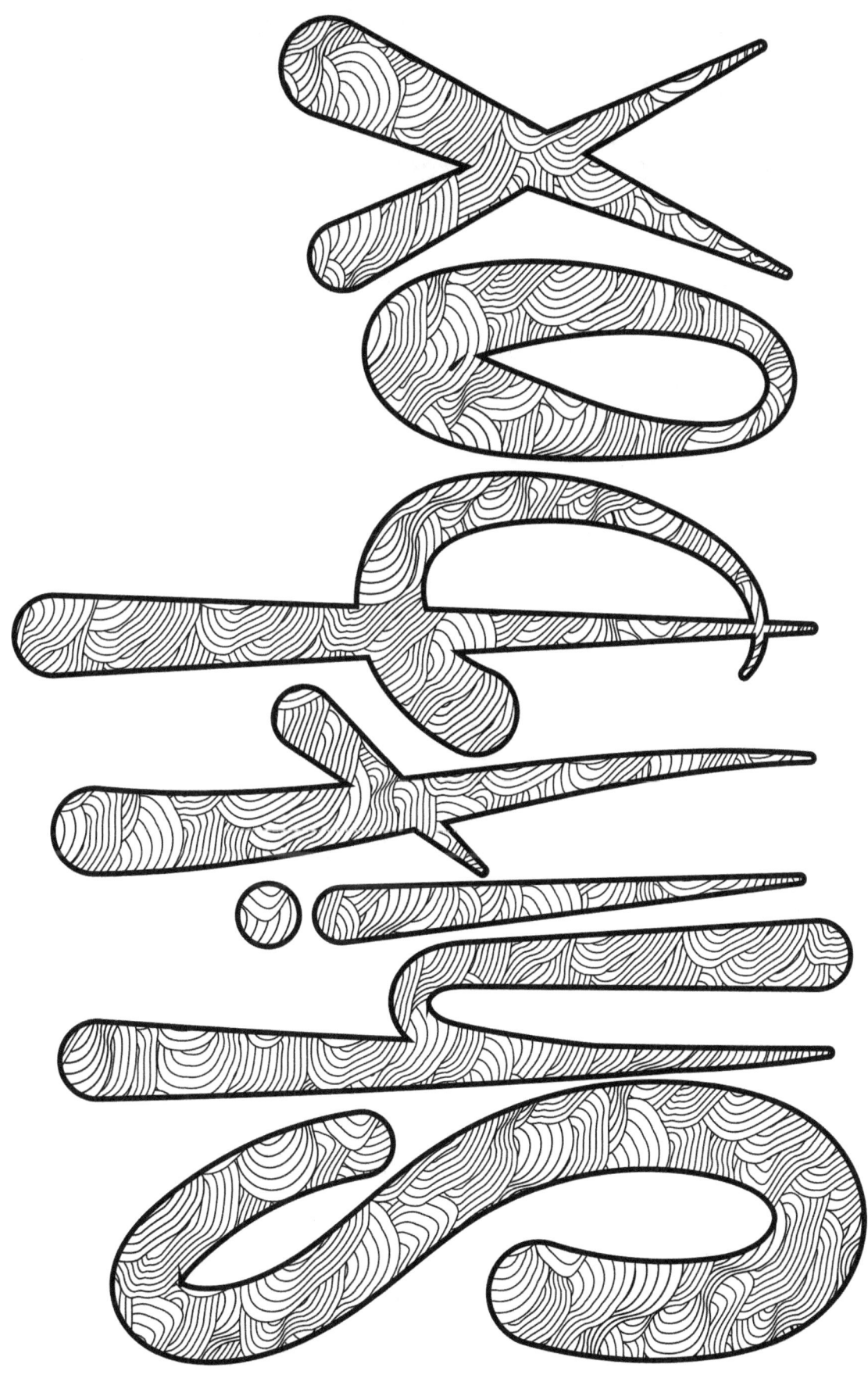

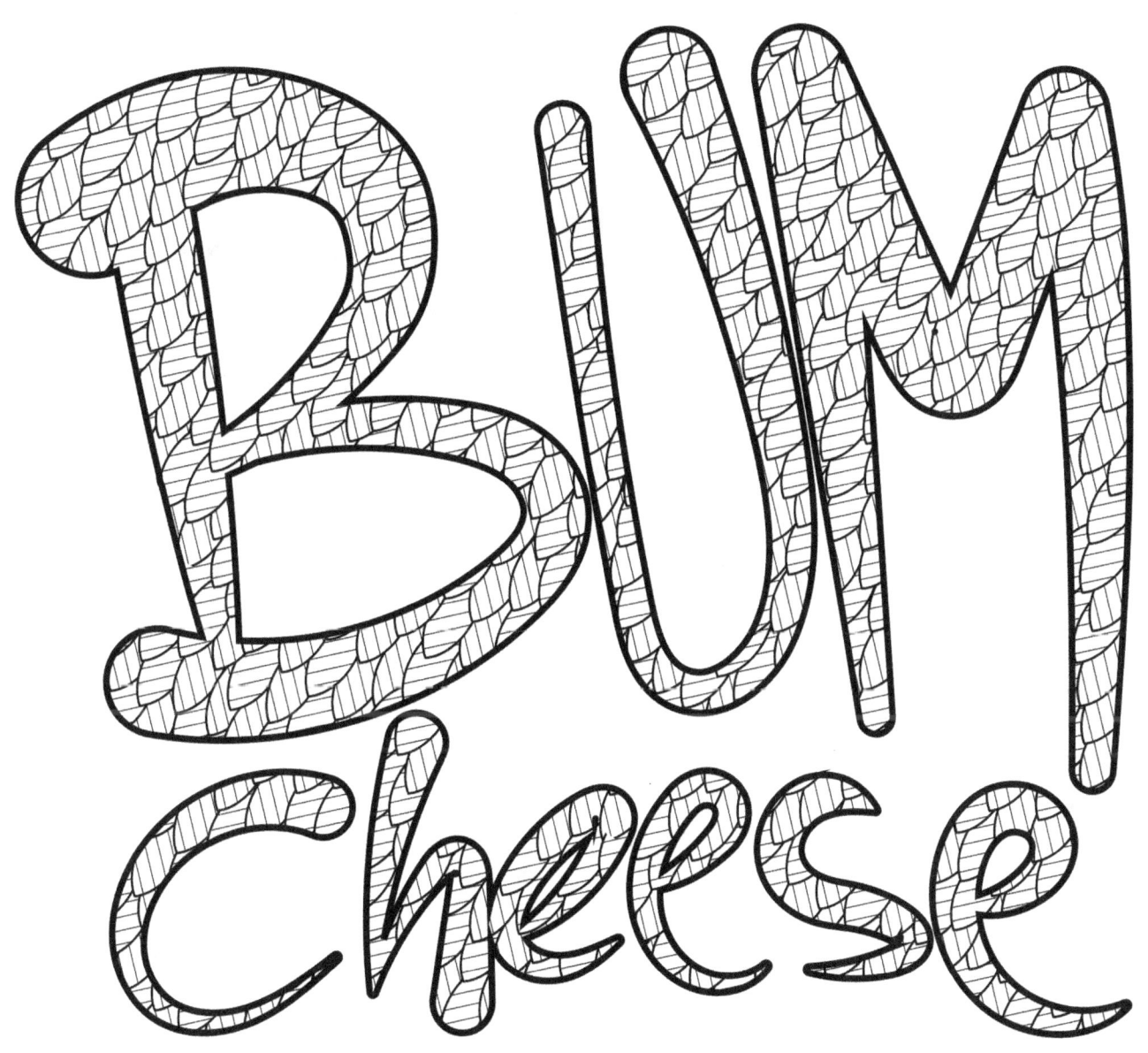

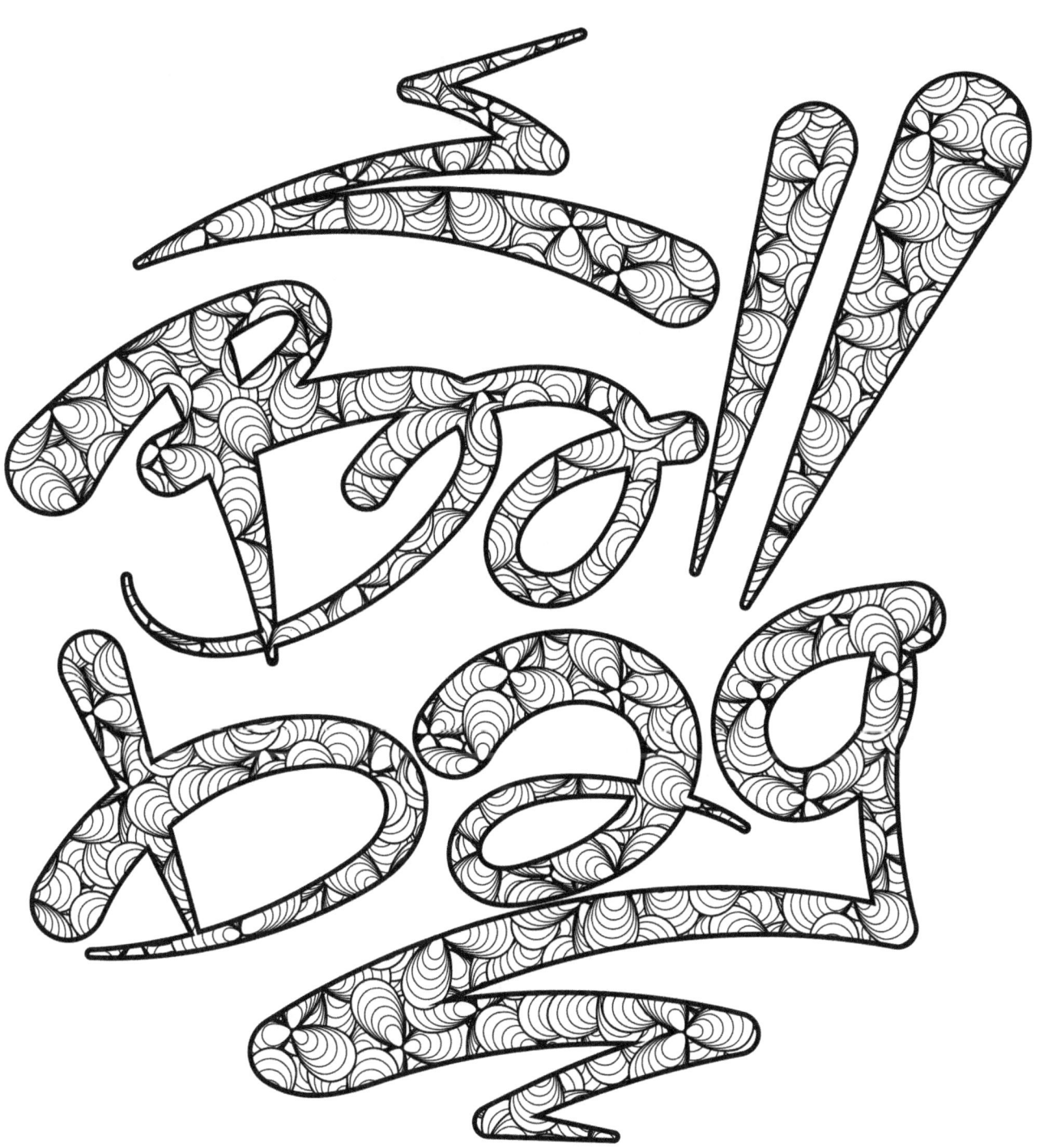

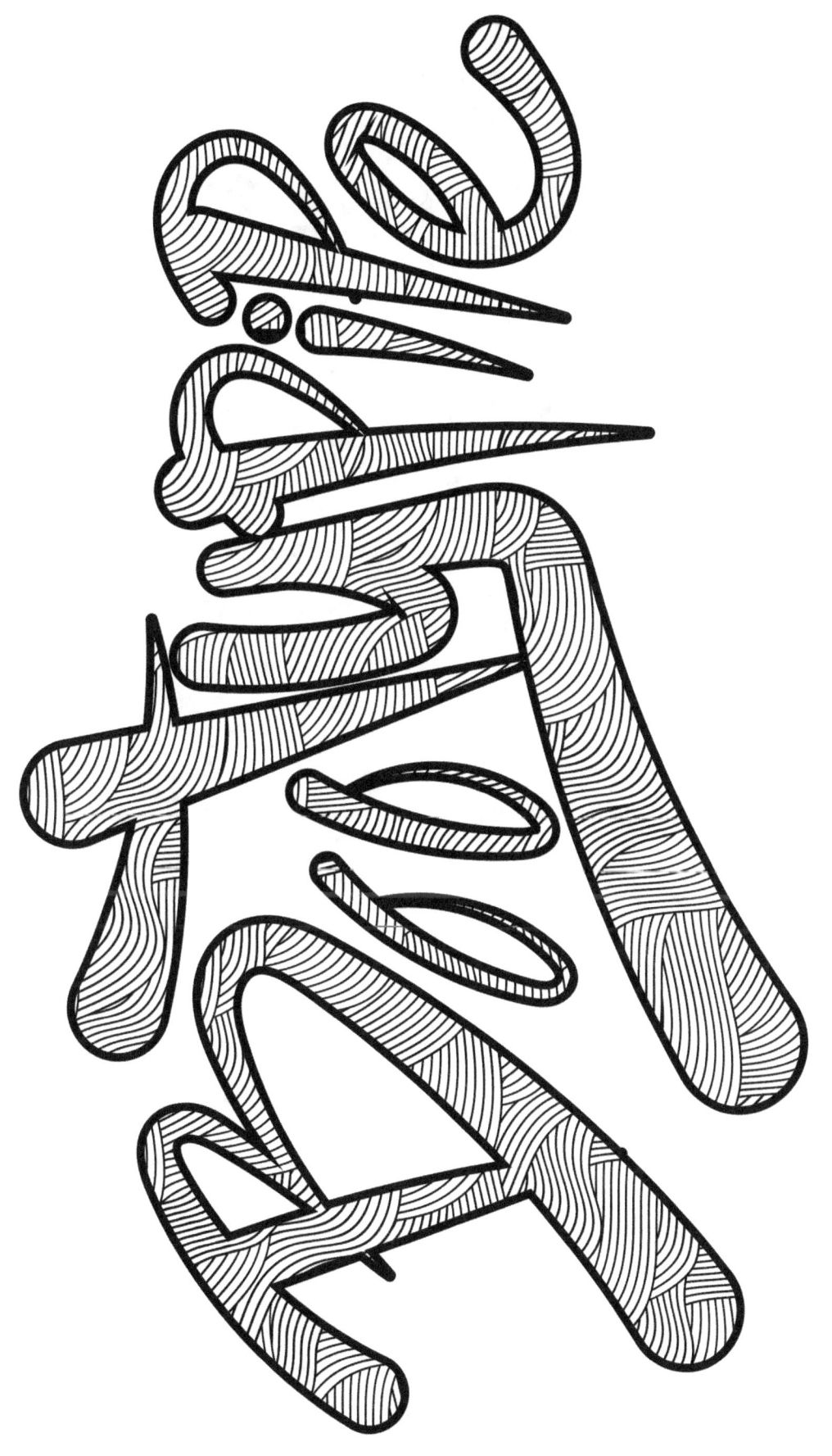

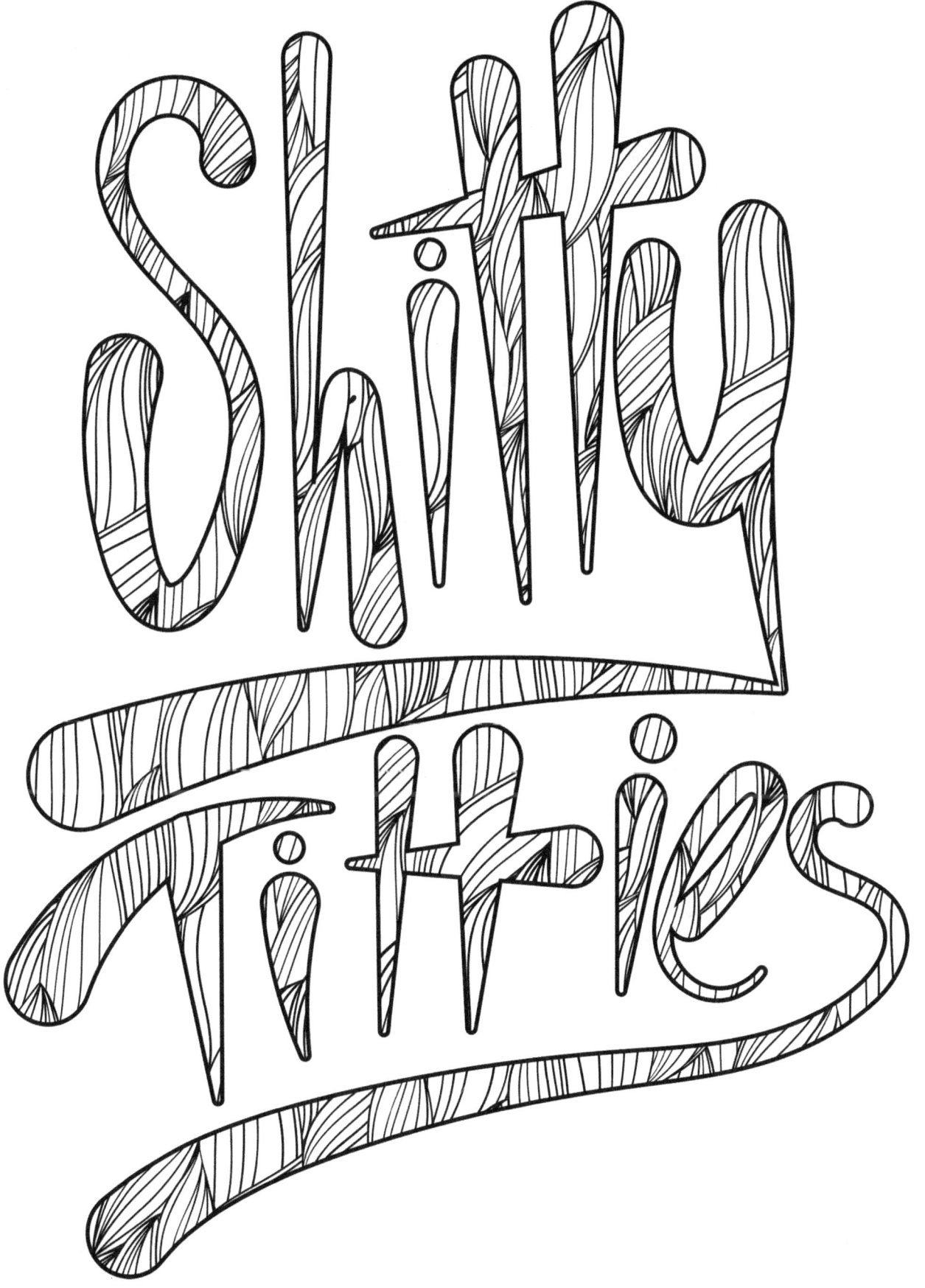

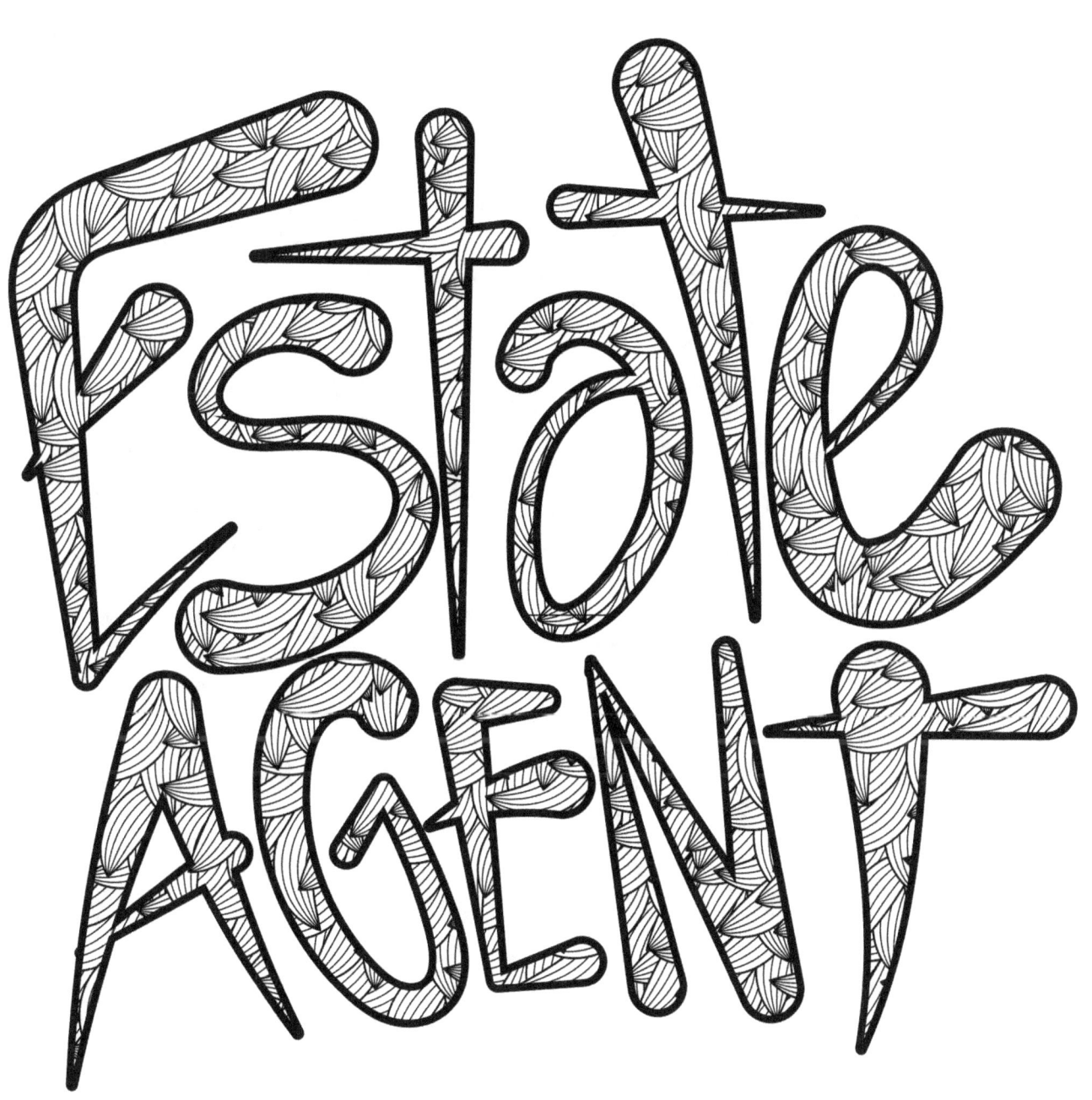

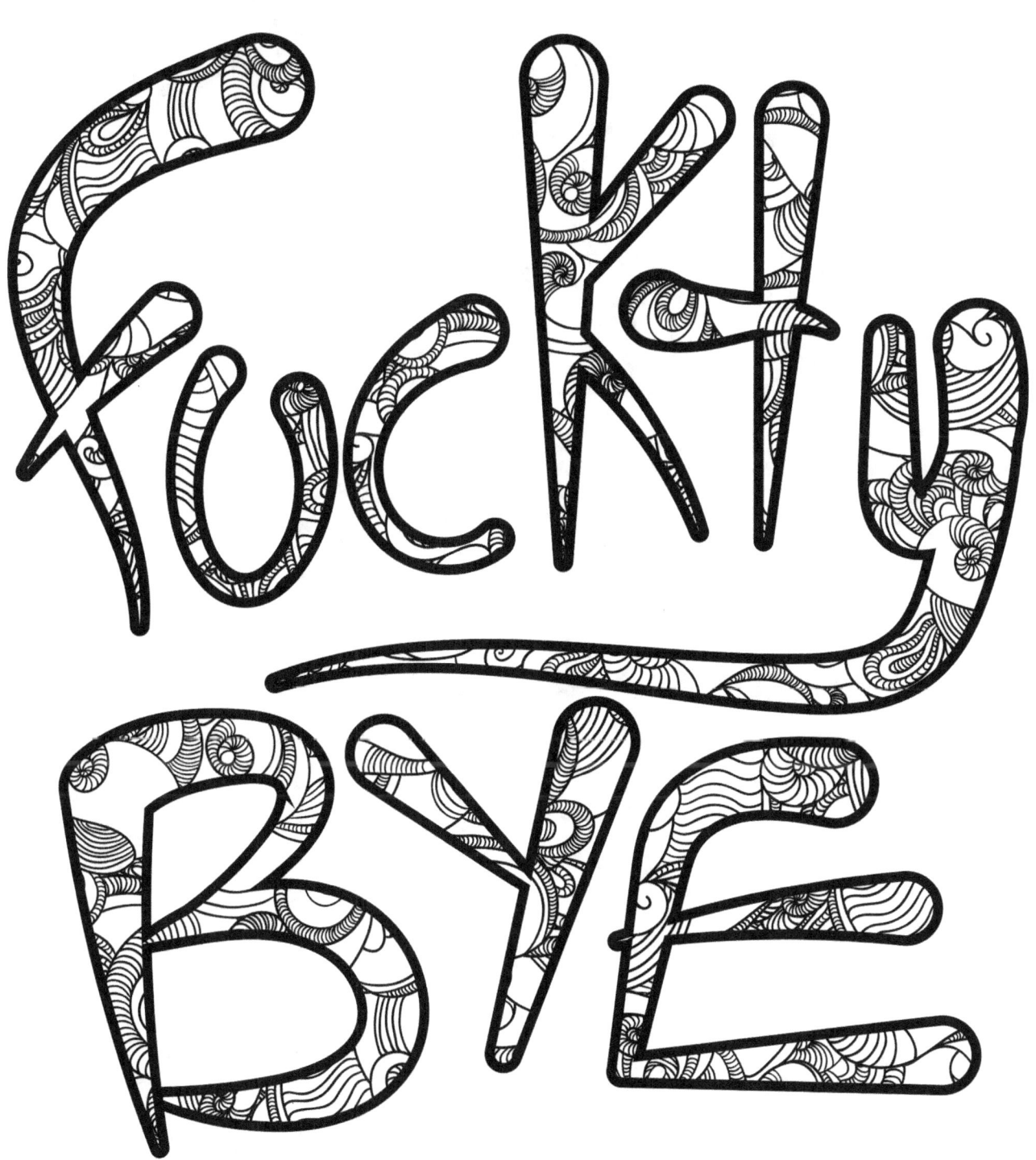

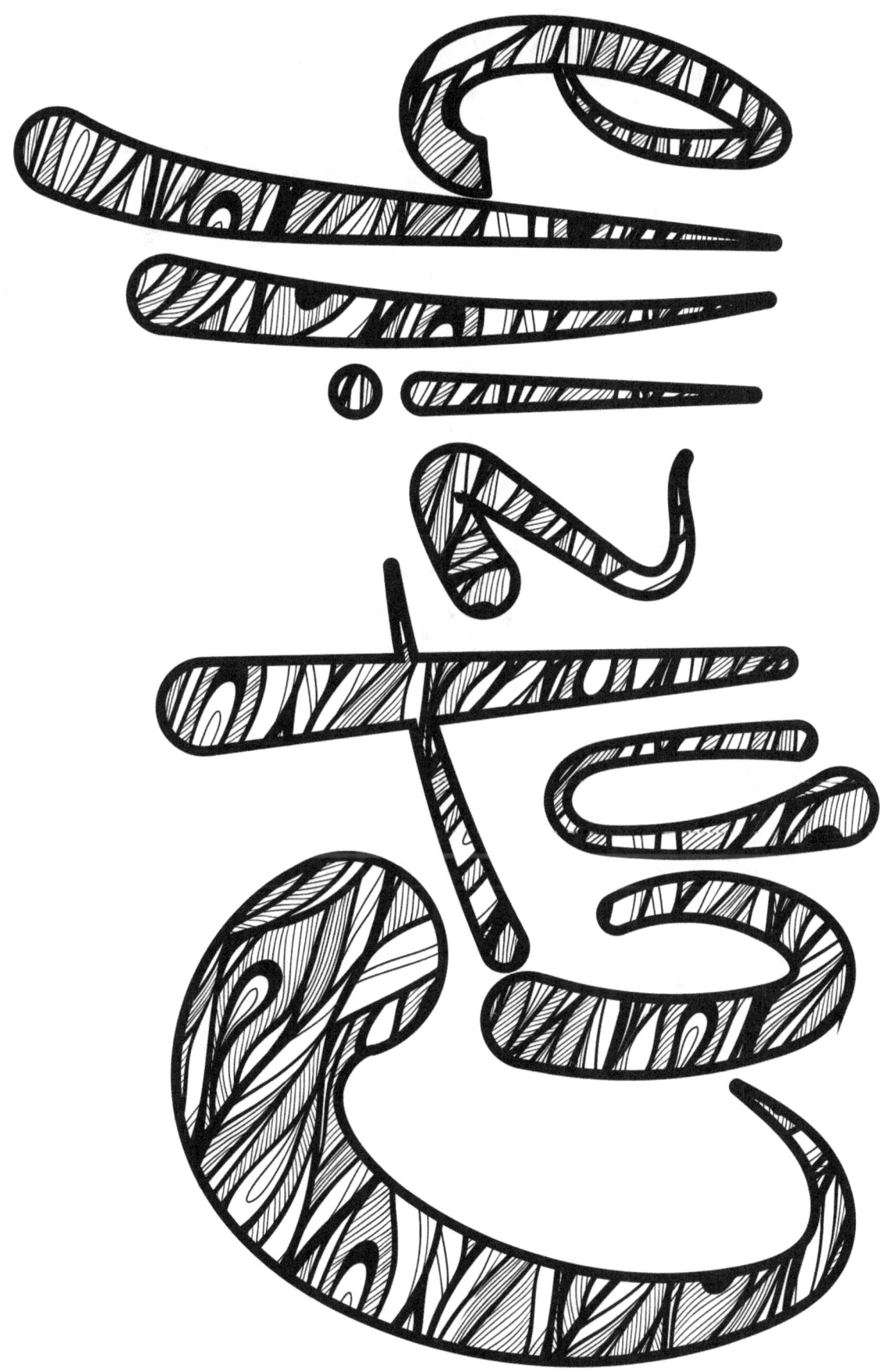

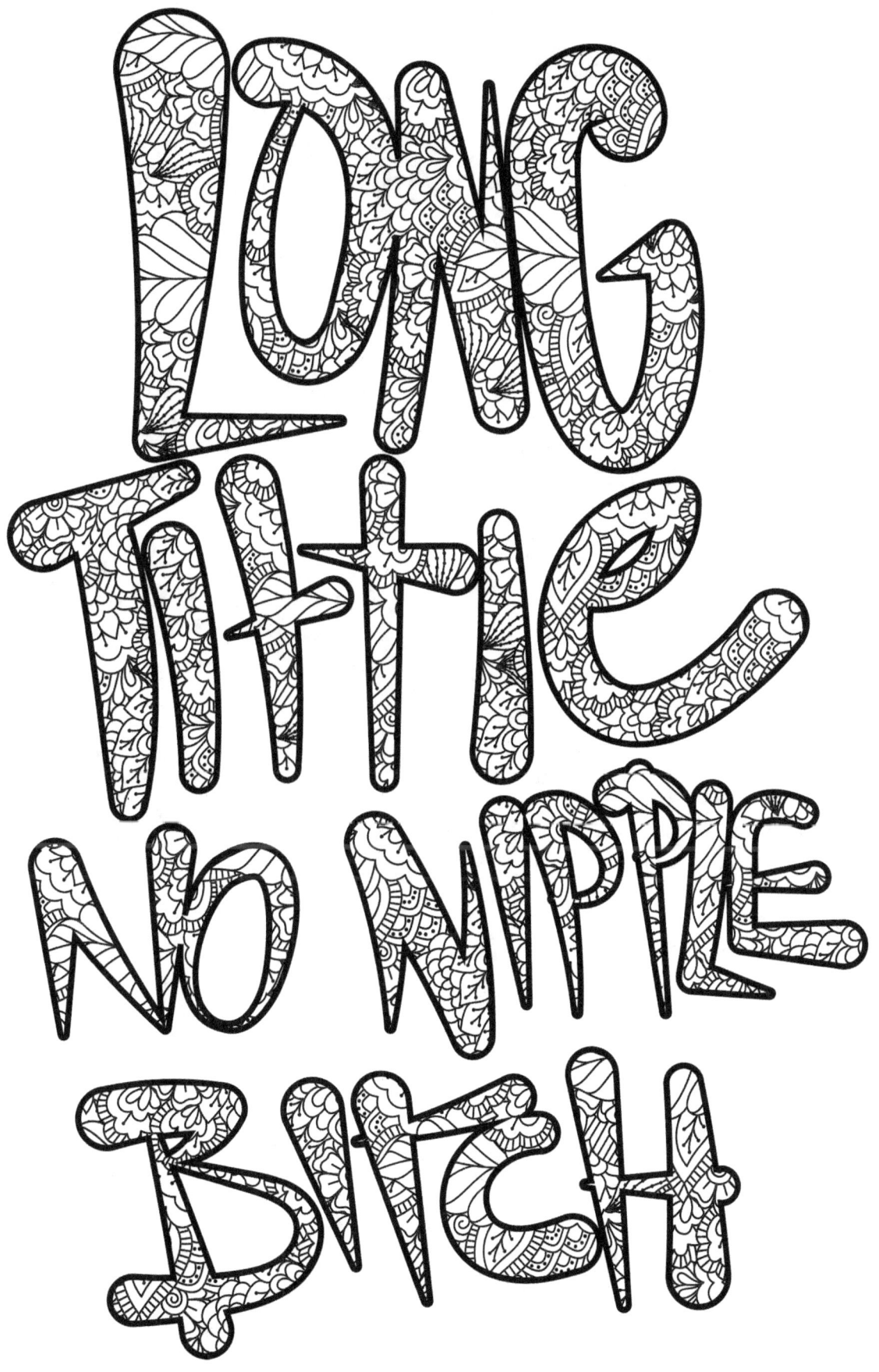

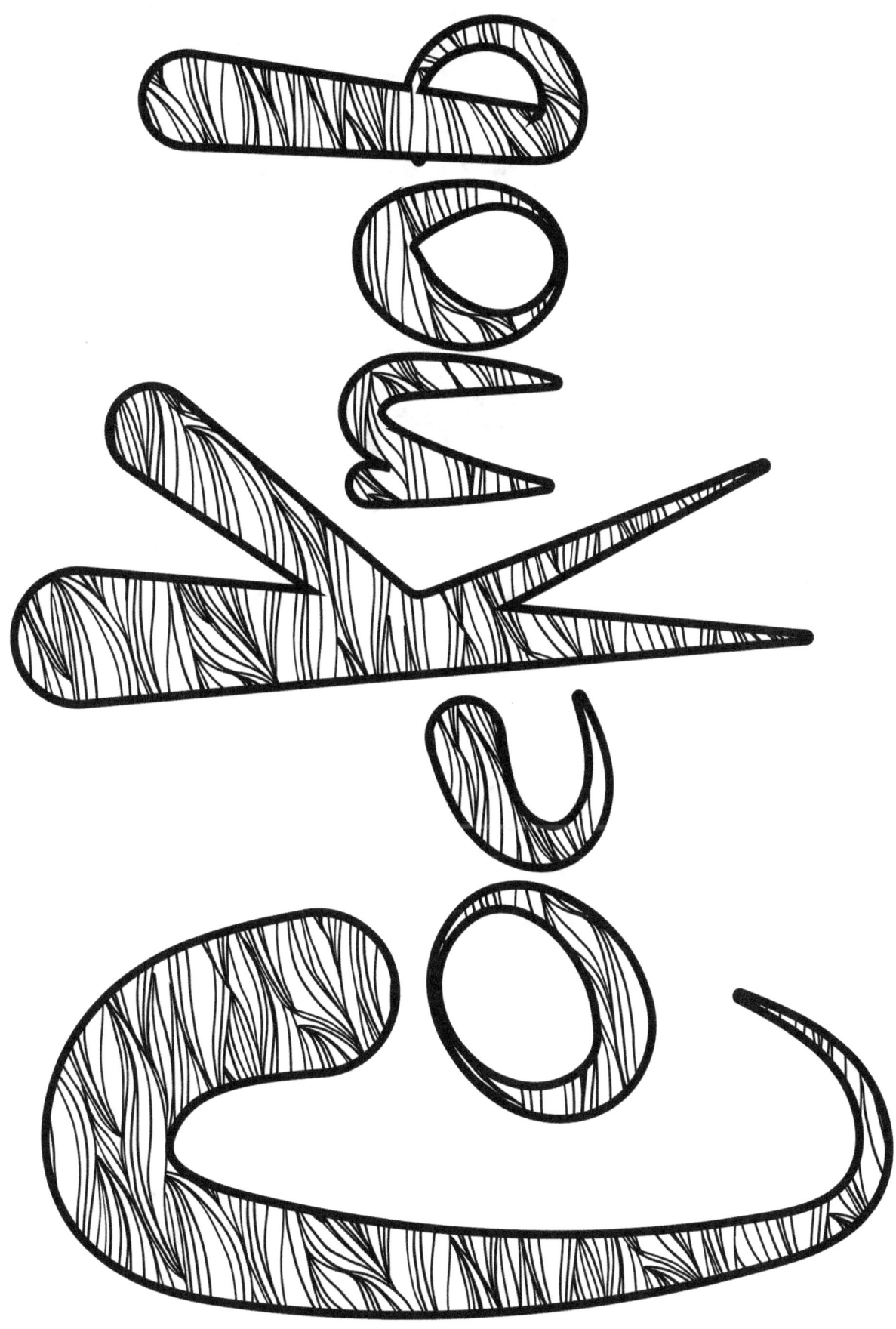

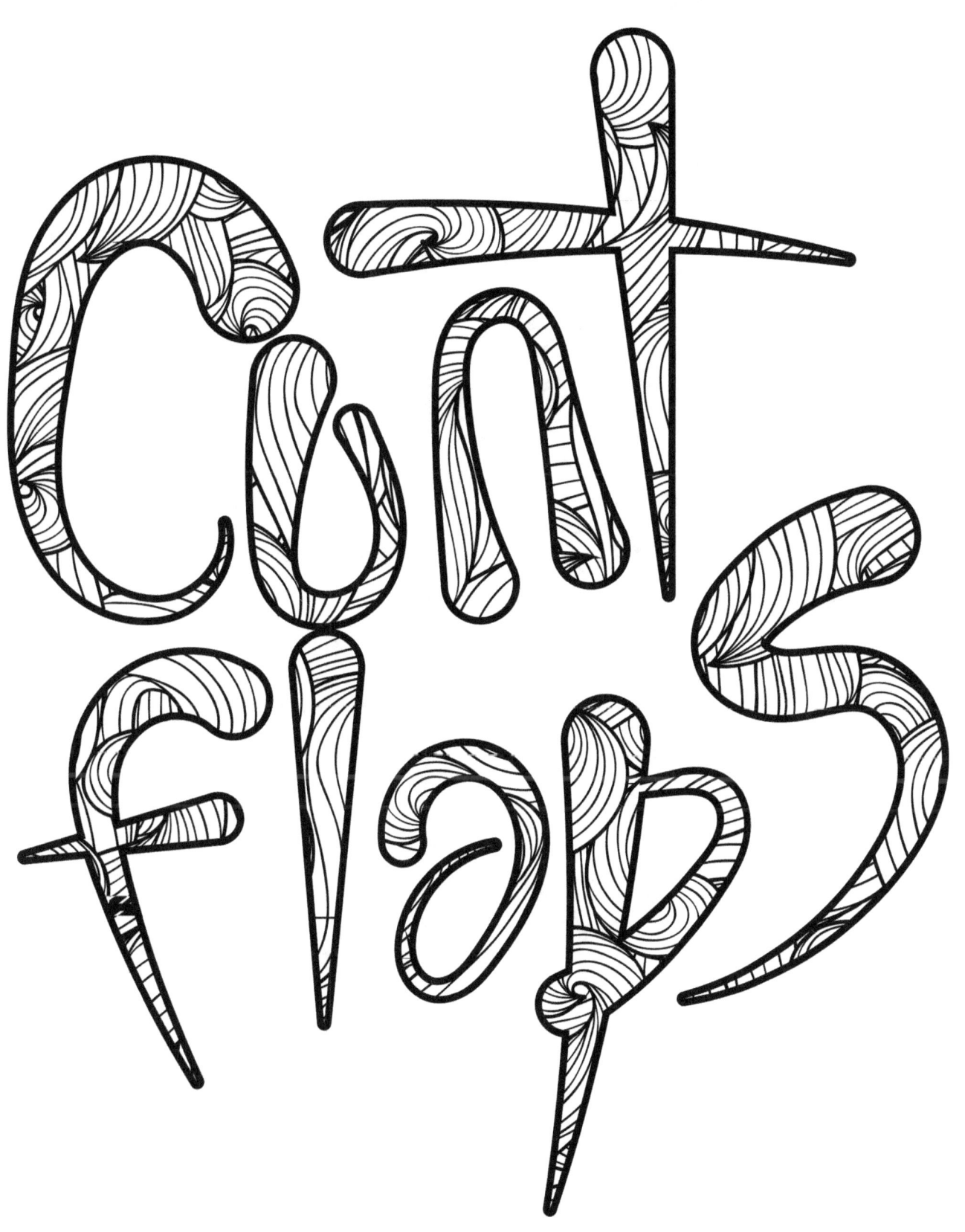

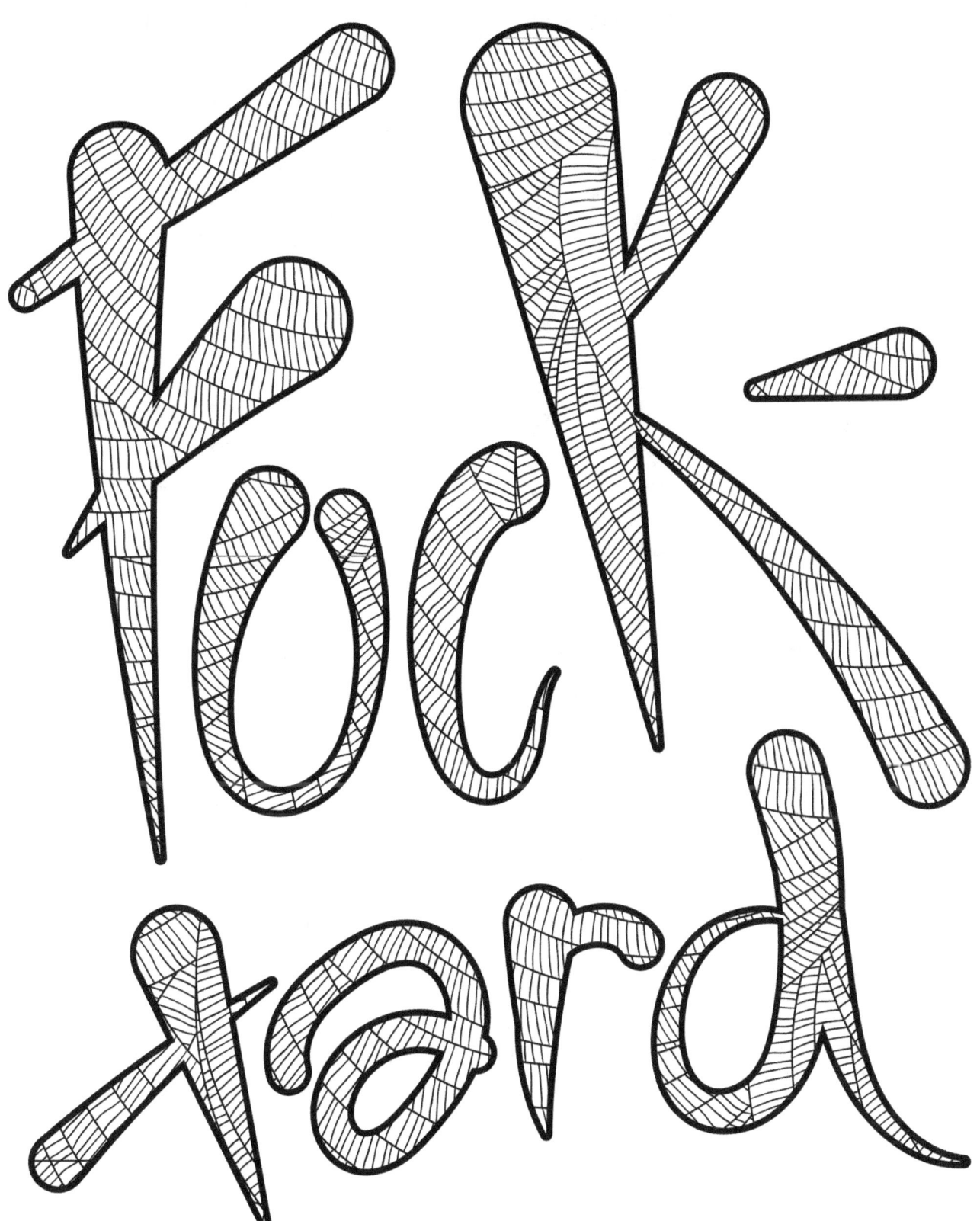

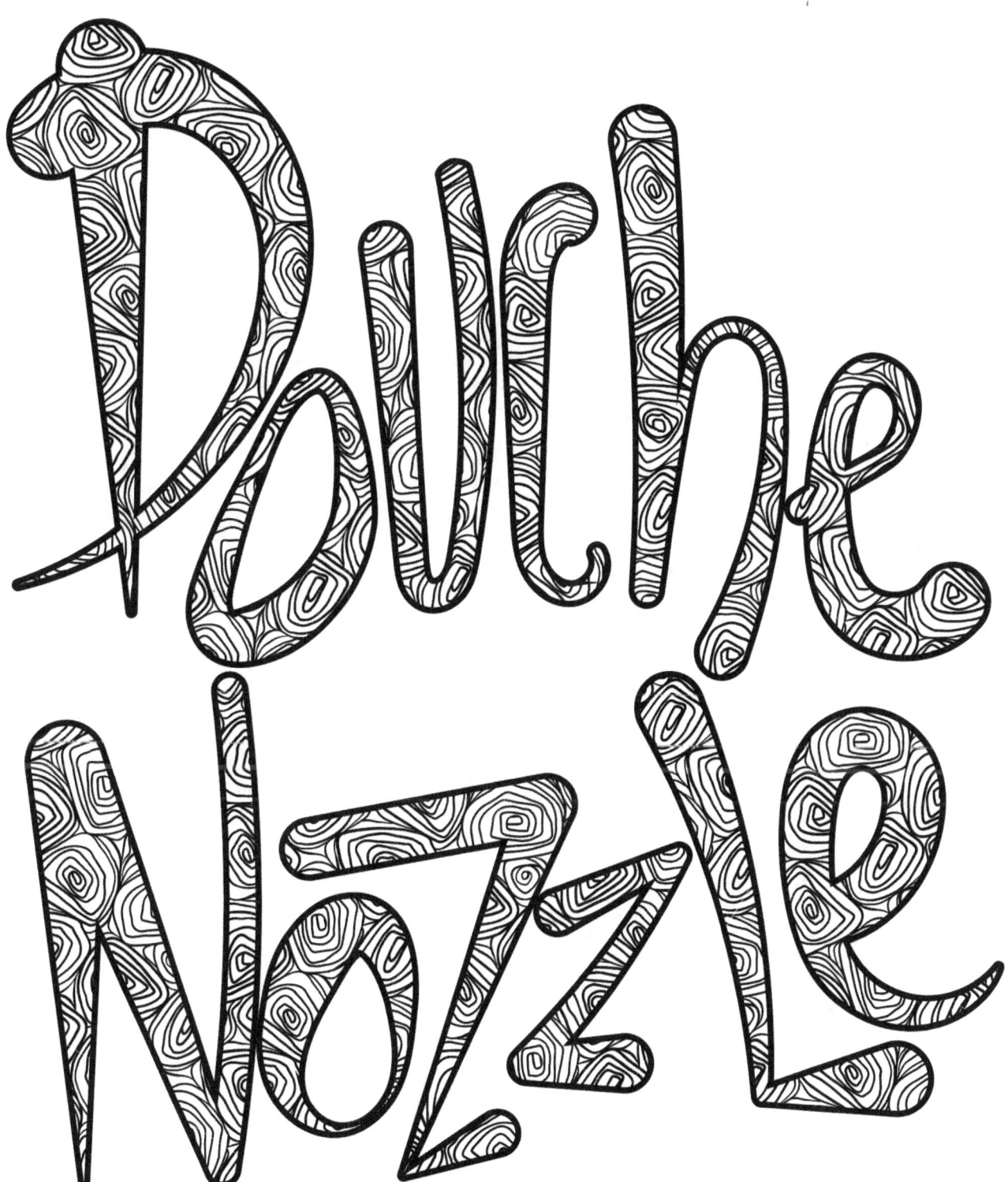

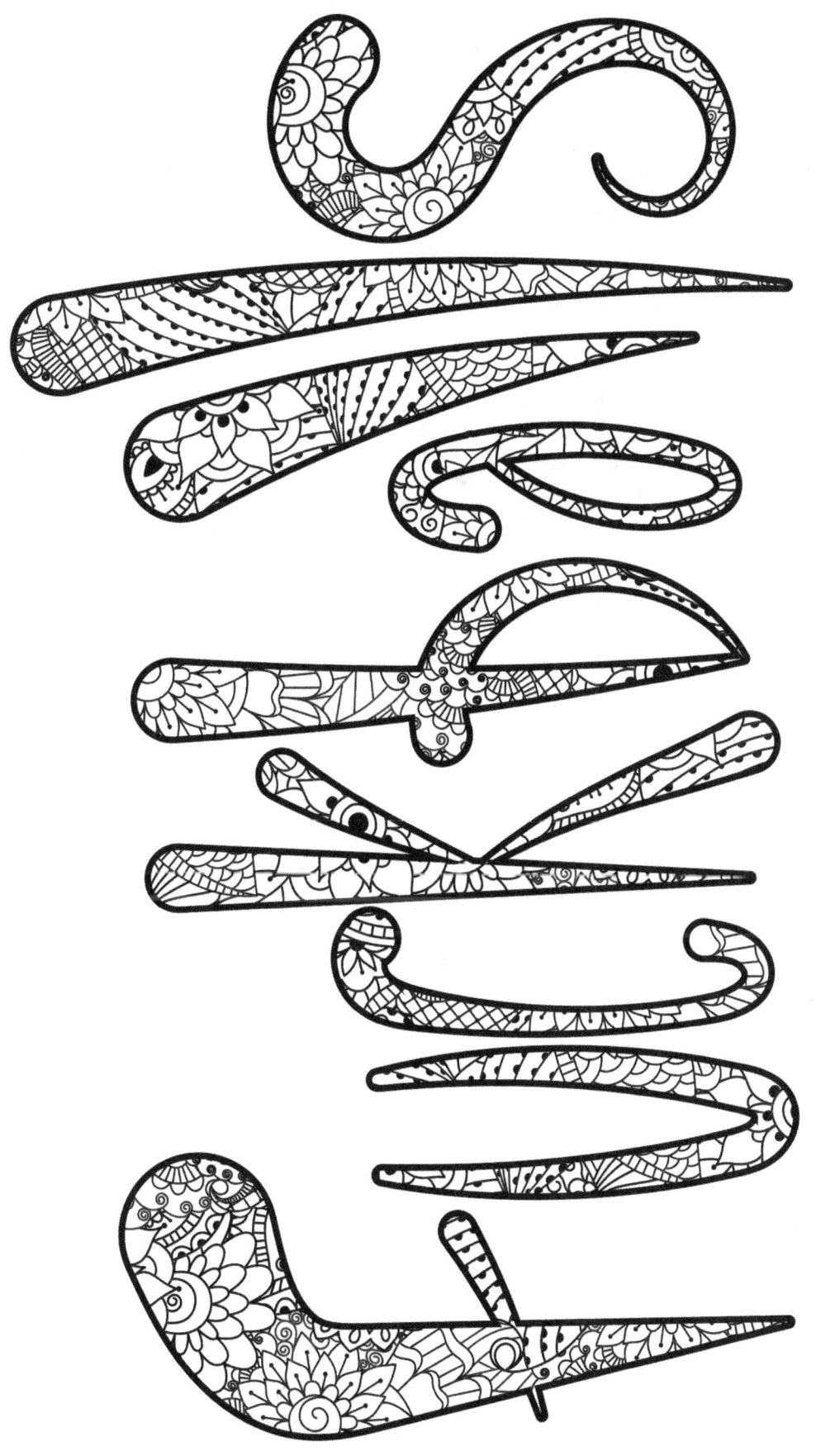

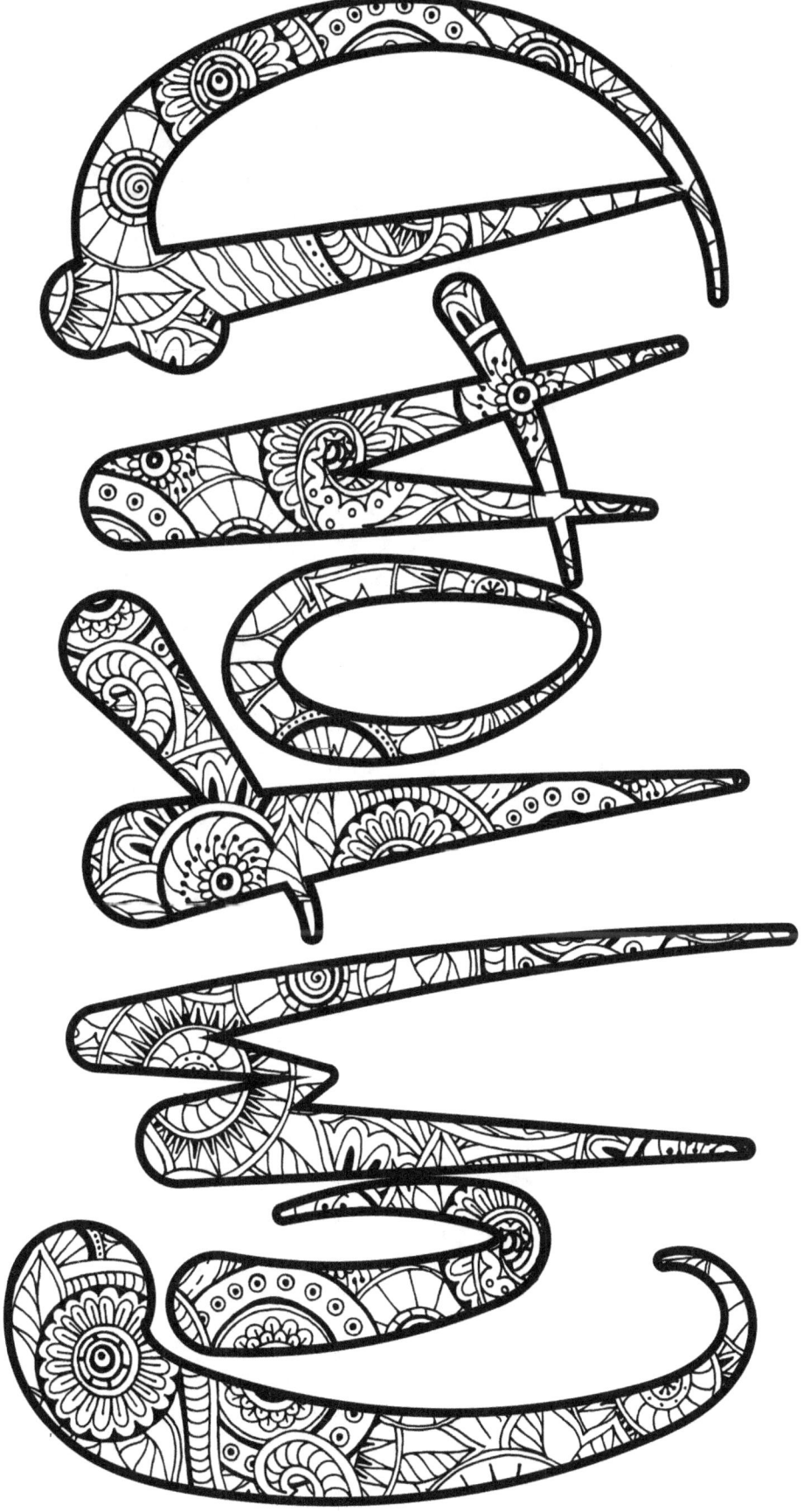

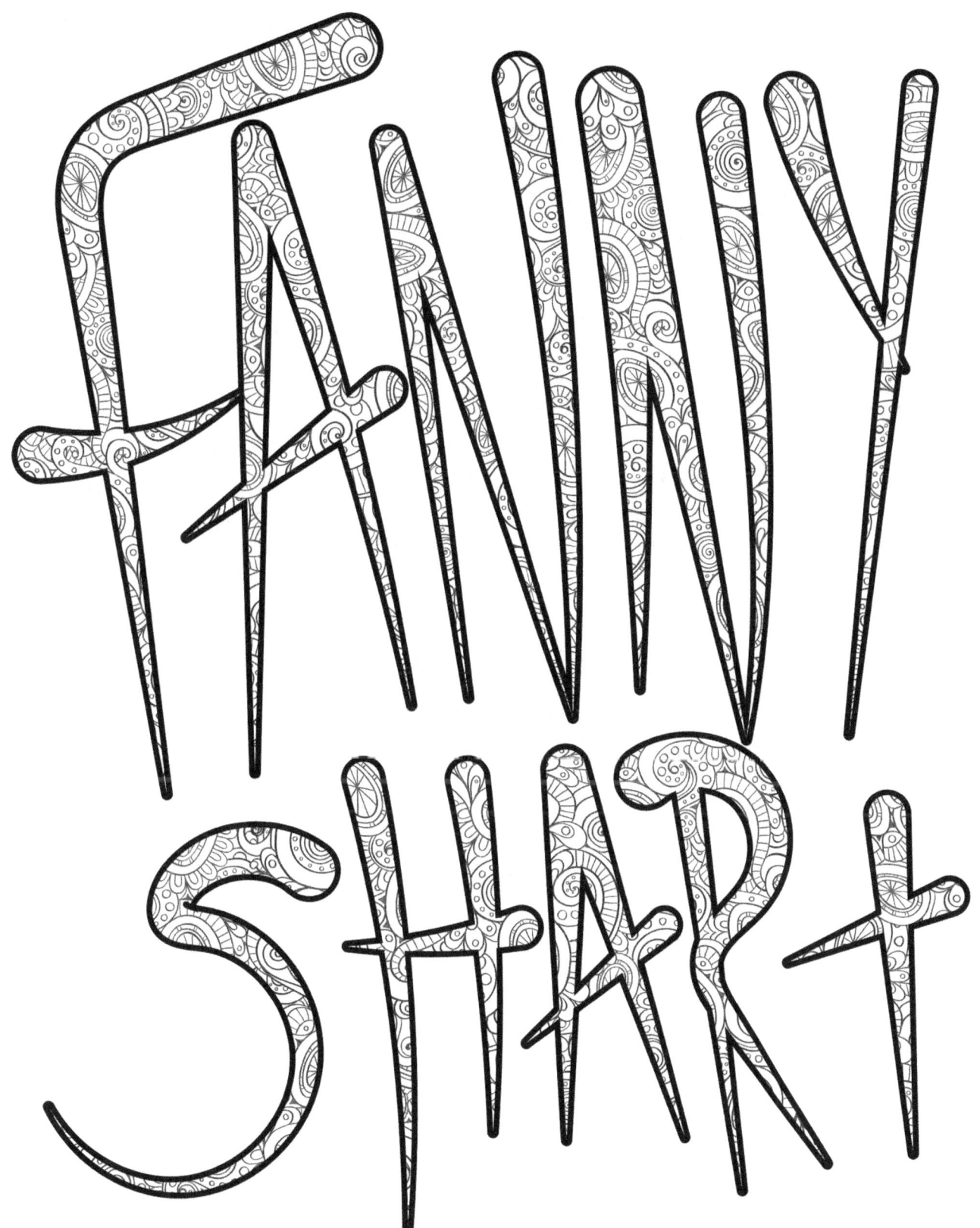

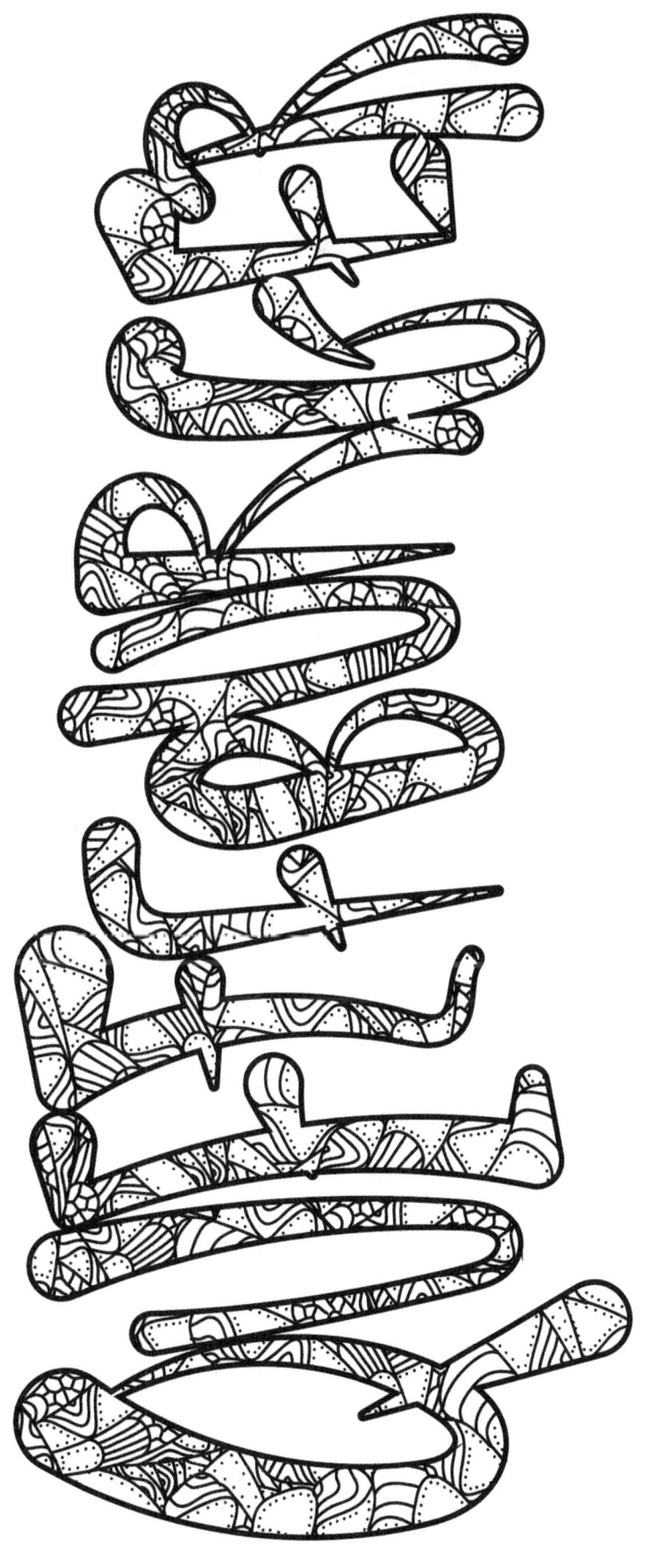

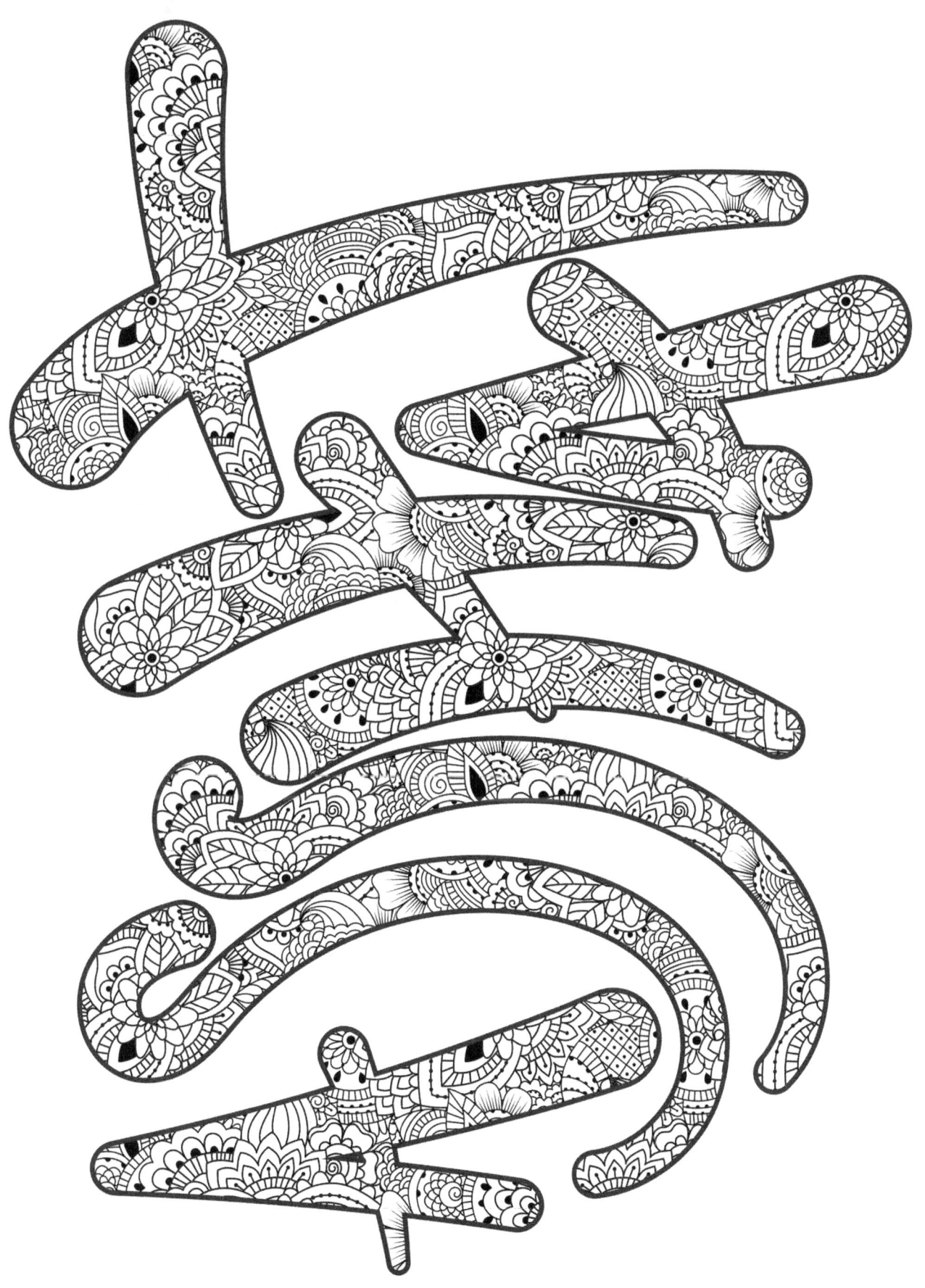

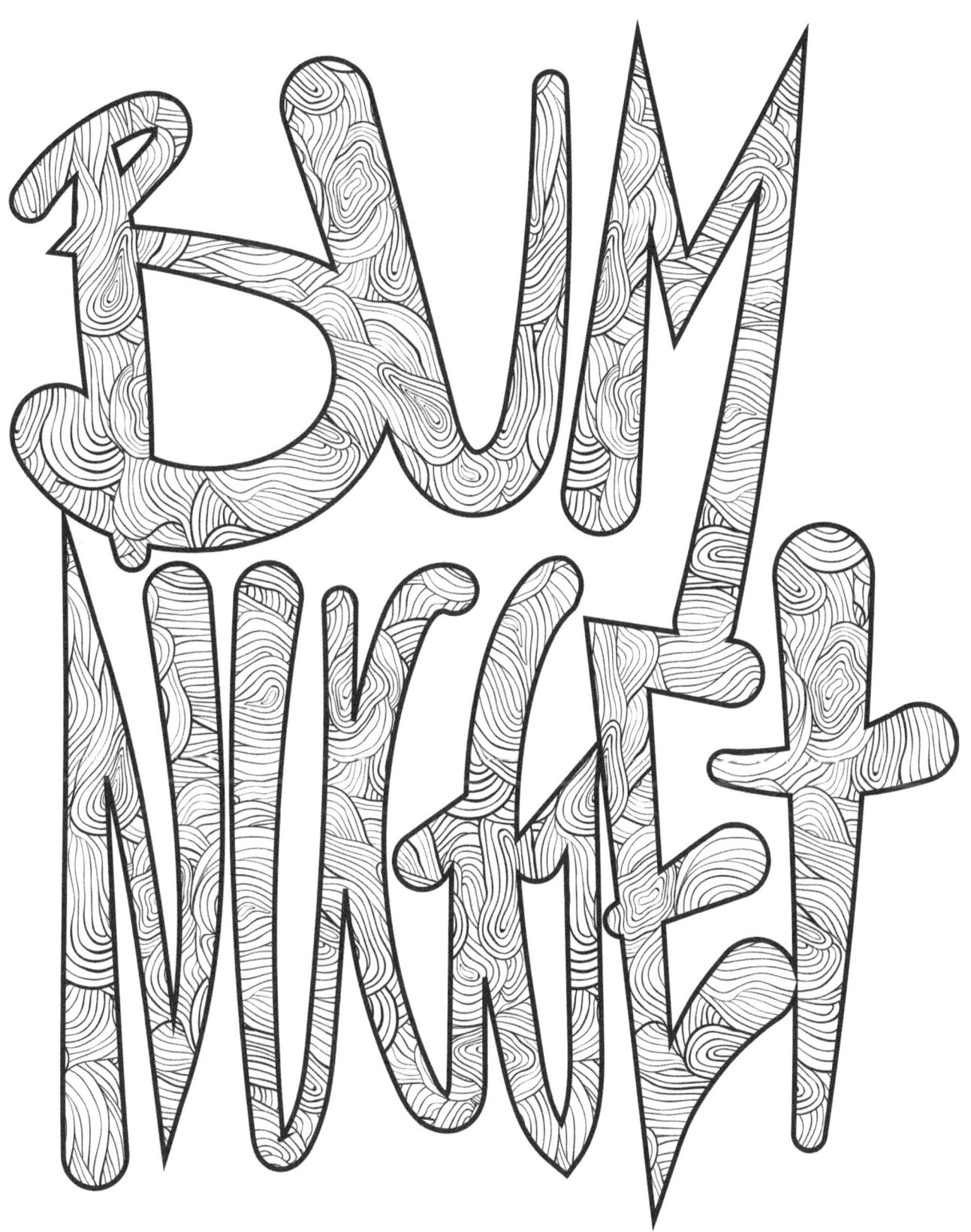

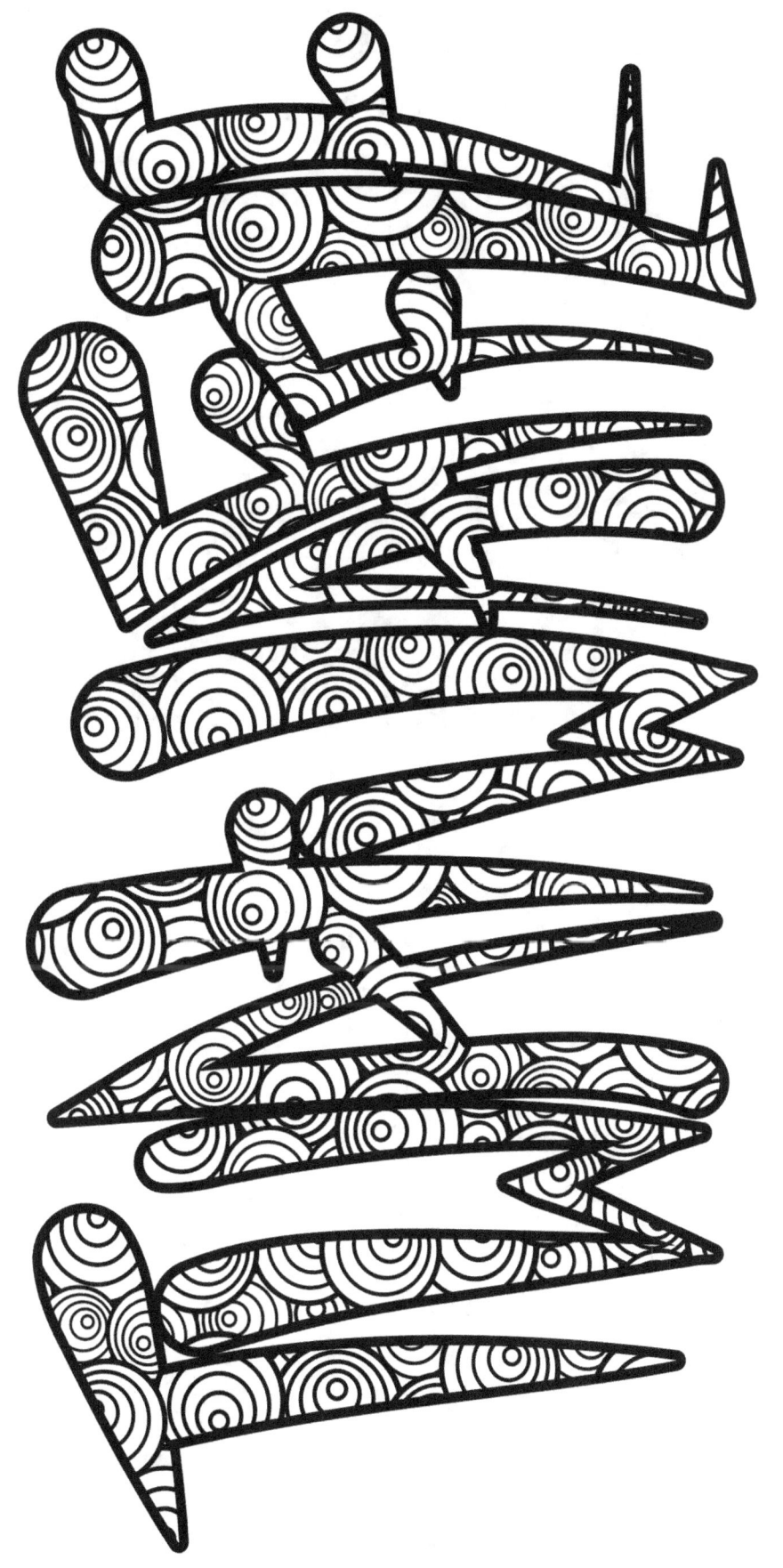

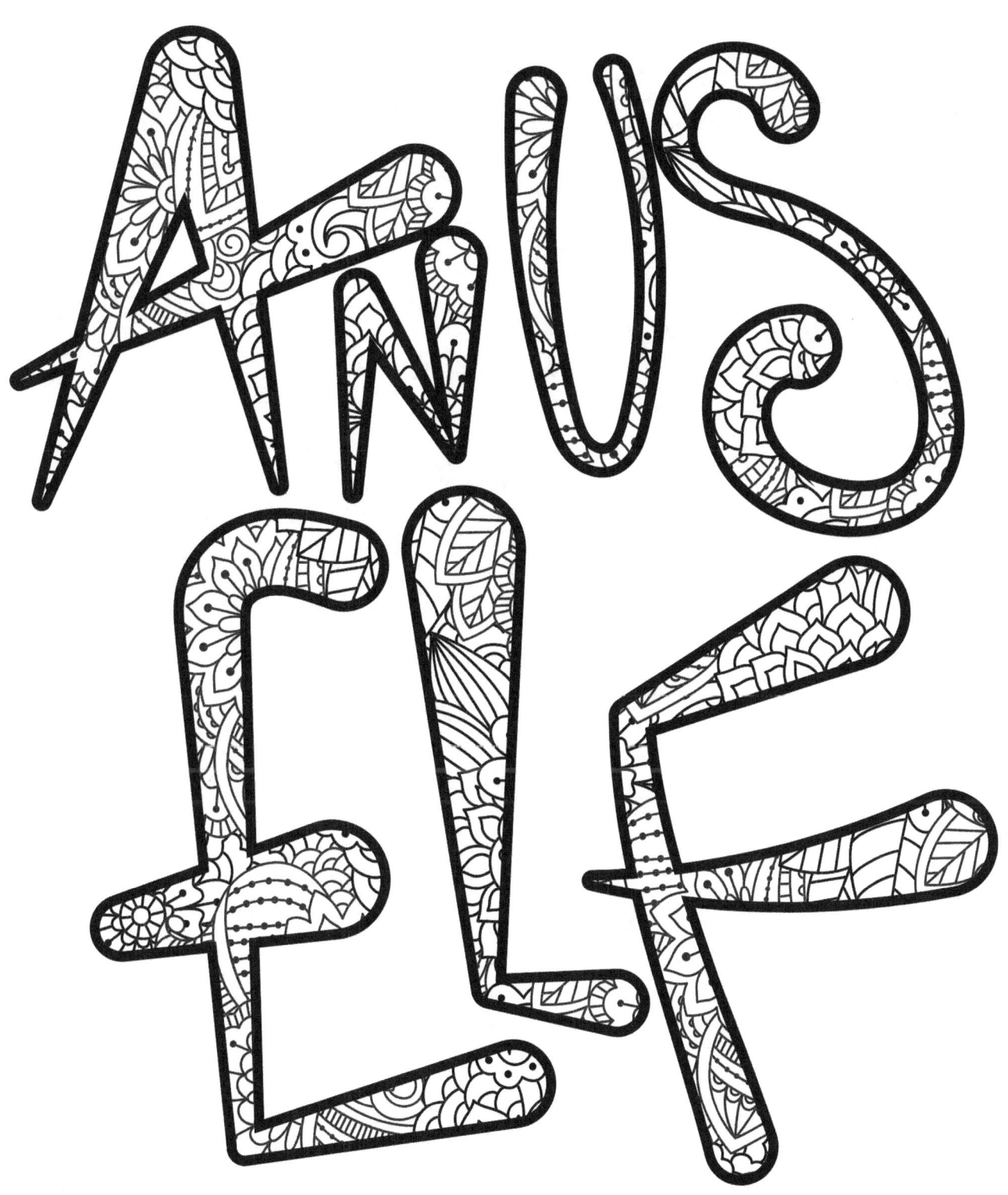

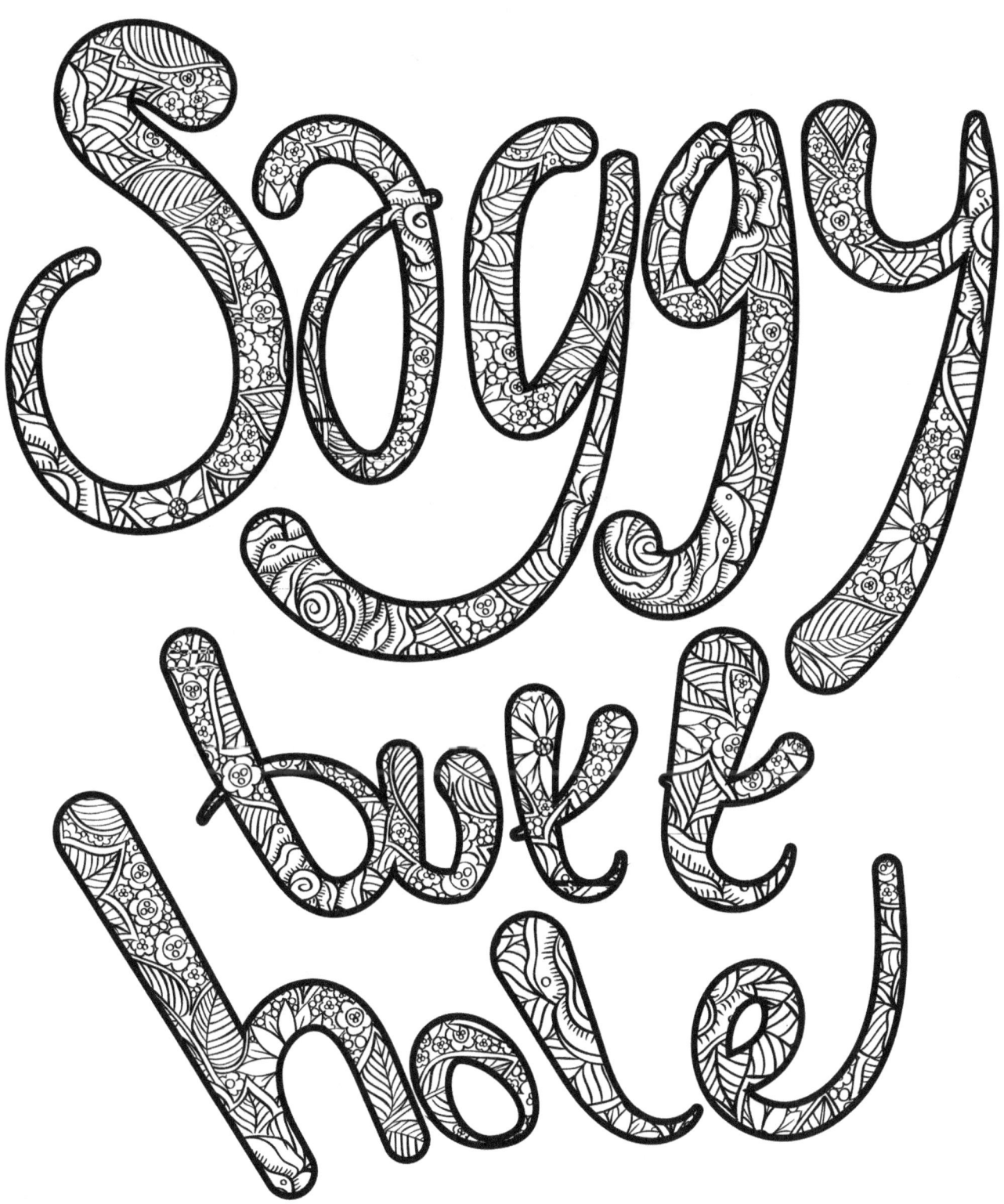

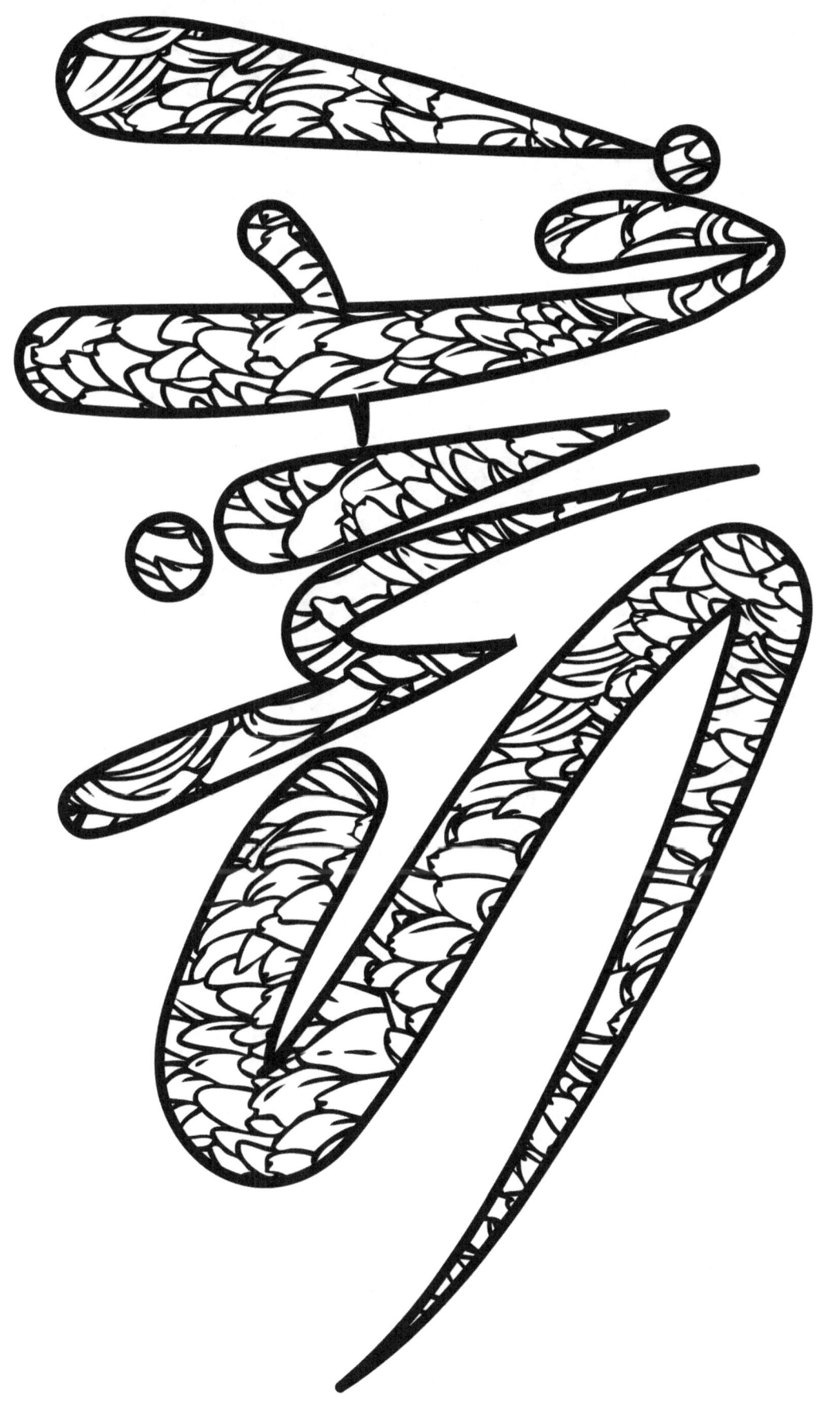

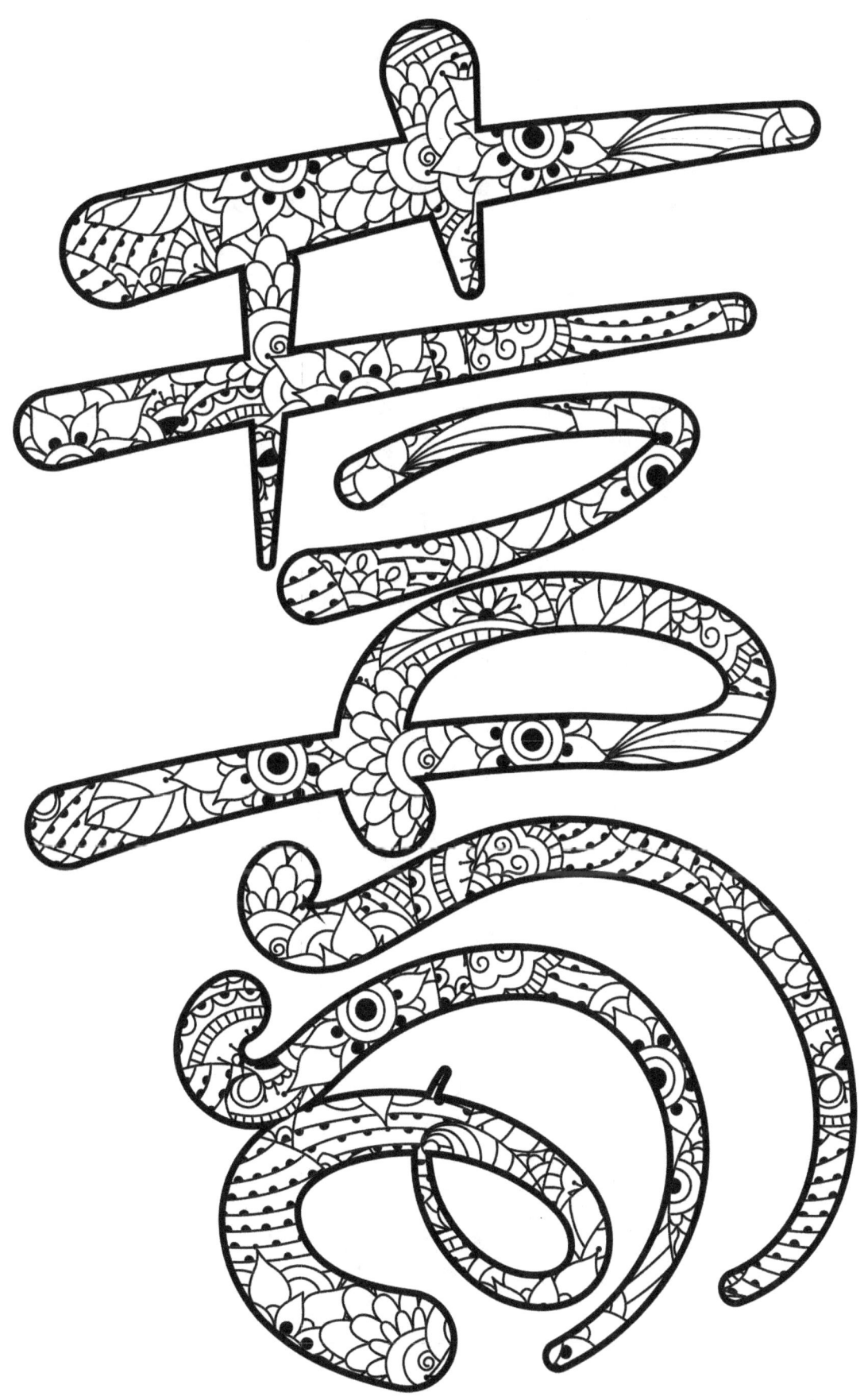

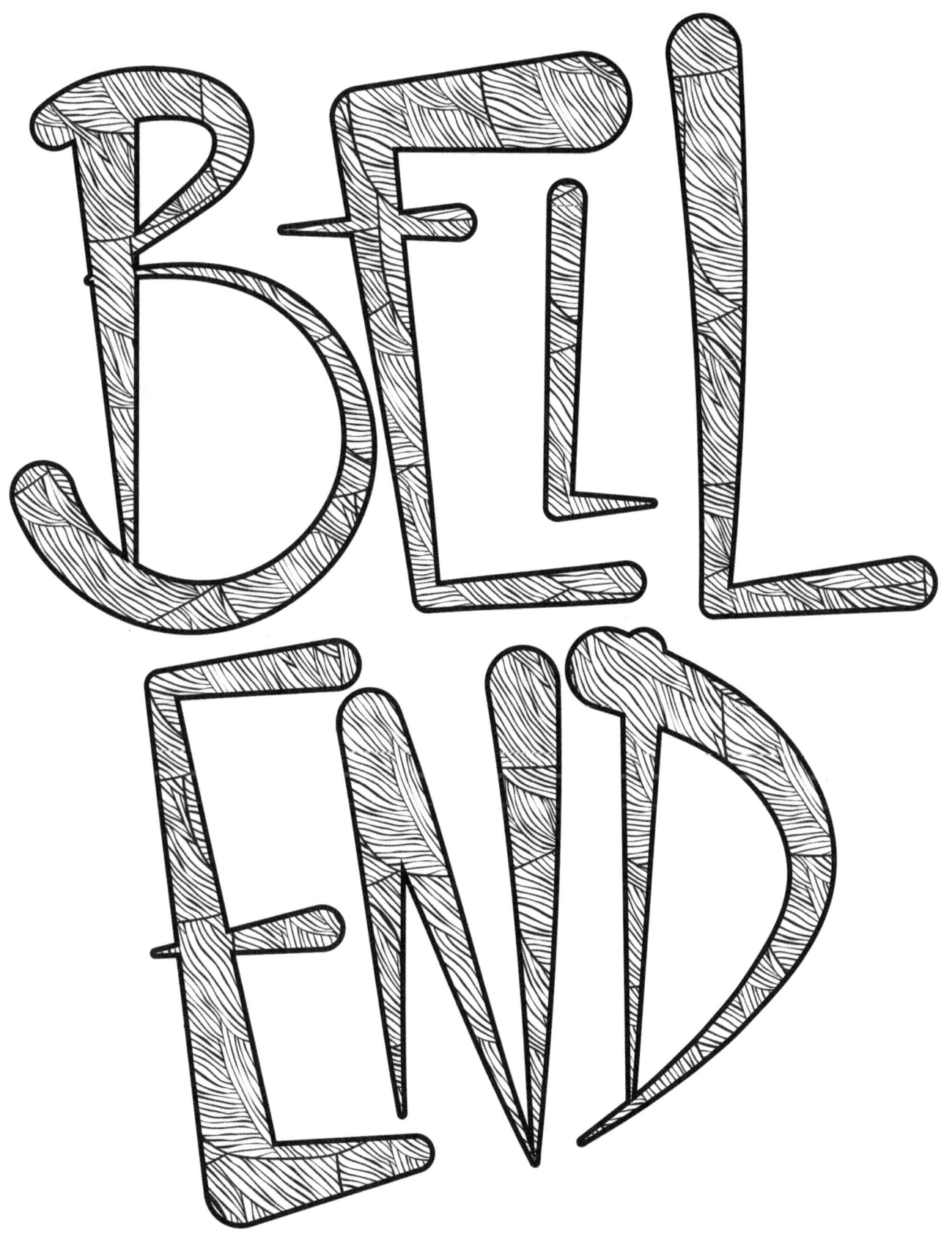

www.ingramcontent.com/pod-product-compliance
Lightning Source LLC
Chambersburg PA
CBHW081210180526
45170CB00006B/2288